STORIES OUT OF SCHOOL

STORIES OUT OF SCHOOL

cribbed by Alvin Stardust
egged on by Arthur Marshall

Quiller Press
London

Fairfield Catering, Fairfield House, 47/51 Kingston Crescent, Portsmouth, Hants. PO2 8QJ. Tel: (0705) 694824

Sutcliffe Catering Group is one of the UK's largest staff catering management companies and part of the P&O group. Their expertise is based on feeding over 1,000,000 people each week at their place of work. Now Sutcliffe are successfully applying these same skills of food excellence and nutritional balance in the provision of food in schools, accelerated by the recent integration of Fairfield Catering in December 1985. Fairfield operate a large number of catering services for schools, colleges and other educational establishments – a far cry from the school dinners of yesteryear!

Quiller Press Ltd.
50 Albemarle Street,
London W1

First published 1986

ISBN 0 907621 79 1

Designed by Jim Reader
Cartoons by Benny Kandler

Design and production in association with
Book Production Consultants, Cambridge

Typeset by The Burlington Press (Cambridge) Ltd, Foxton, Cambridge
Printed and bound by Billing & Sons Ltd, Worcester

Contents

Foreword

When I first went to boarding school I was relatively anonymous to the general public and a complete non event to many, so to be recognised was usually a surprising experience. School expeditions were perhaps more interesting for me than almost anybody else due to my comparatively sheltered upbringing! One such expedition took us to Canterbury Cathedral where there were several other schools present.

A group of schoolboys came over and much to my surprise asked me for my autograph, an unknown phenomenon. But – I knew it wasn't allowed so I'm afraid I used an excuse which you can't use often. I took the book and put a little cross – after puzzled looks and a query – 'what's that?' – I looked very apologetic and said, 'I'm very sorry – I can't write.' Curiously enough they seemed to accept that with what I hope was a degree of sympathetic understanding! Even if they did return to their mates shaking their heads.

School dances were always a problem – and you know those days when nothing seems to be going your way? An in-house school dance was one of those occasions.

The visiting school was late and the band didn't turn up and being naive and helpful I went off to put on some music, to find, when I got back, that they were one boy short – and guess who had the prospect of a long lonely evening as even the accompanying Master had been appropriated? Quite incidentally, I don't think any of the visitors knew who I was. I knew from experience that once paired off there was no chance that anyone would let go of their respective partners, well not voluntarily. I came up with a good plan, a dance called the Paul Jones designed to swop partners – it was introduced into the programme and my evening improved dramatically. After my experiences at school dances, any social occasion I've been to since then has been a real party!

My own experiences pale into insignificance beside some of those

7

included in this book and I thank everyone who has contributed a story for their unselfish help on behalf of the many children who will benefit from their revelations and remembrances.

*A**nne***

HRH The Princess Anne
President, Save the Children

Introduction

I believe this is the most comprehensive collection of stories about English schools which has been put together this century – and probably ever. It covers public schools, state schools, nursery schools, convent schools and army schools and describes almost every printable aspect of education I could think of.

When Serena Kellie asked me if I would edit a book of 'Stories out of school' for The Save the Children Fund, I did not want to collect just another joke book of celebrities' anecdotes – although I hope the fun side of school life is well covered here. I felt that the subject deserved digging a little deeper into the seam.

Of course, there are several general books about school life – but they tend to concentrate on one kind of school, usually the boy's public school. Indeed, to read all the literature you would think every Tom, Dick and Harry (not to mention Harriet) went to a public school. You would also be led to believe that the average English boy spent his entire schooldays being cruelly mistreated by his seniors and/or being the subject of sexual attack. Almost all published memoirs of the past twenty-five years appear to feel obliged to delve into these topics in considerable detail. In this selection of recollections, we have attempted to put *that* side of school life into perspective.

This means that we have explored the various other aspects of school life just as fully, and we have dealt with the 'Funny Ha! Ha!' as well as the 'Funny peculiar'. Strangely enough, it was not easy to find good examples of the former, as most of my friends don't seem to have found their schooldays particularly amusing. Ex-schoolmasters and present-day staff, on the other hand, seem to find a lot to laugh about.

To all those who supplied me with anecdotes, whether friends, or teachers and pupils who wrote about incidents at school – to them all I send hearty thanks. I am also grateful to Serena Kellie who did much of the contact work, and to Peter King and publisher Jeremy Greenwood who have keenly sought material from here, there and everywhere.

At the end of the book we have listed all the names of those who helped us produce this book, as well as authors and publishers who gave us permission for quotations from their work to be used. The illustrator Benny Kandler has also done a great job. I know that The Save the Children Fund joins with me in saying a big thank you to everyone who has helped, especially of course our sponsor, Sutcliffe Catering, and their specialist schools division, Fairfield Catering..

It only remains for me to ask all my readers to recommend the book to their friends and relations, their fellow pupils, former pupils, staff and ex-staff, so that the sales of the book will bring a substantial sum of money, in royalties, to that splendid cause, The Save the Children Fund.

Alvin Standust

June 1986

The village master

Beside yon straggling fence that skirts the way,
With blossom'd furze unprofitably gay,
There, in his noisy mansion, skilled to rule,
The village master taught his little school;
A man severe he was, and stern to view;
I knew him well, and every truant knew;
Well had the boding tremblers learn'd to trace,
The day's disasters in his morning face;
Full well they laugh'd, with counterfeited glee,
At all his jokes, for many a joke had he;
Full well the busy whisper, circling round,
Convey'd the dismal tidings when he frowned;
Yet he was kind; or if severe in aught,
The love he bore to learning was in fault;
The village all declared how much he knew;
'Twas certain he could write, and cypher too;
Lands he could measure, terms and tides presage,
And even the story ran that he could gauge.
In arguing too, the parson own'd his skill,
For e'en though vanquish'd, he could argue still;
While words of learned length and thundering sound
Amaz'd the gazing rustics rang'd around,
And still they gaz'd, and still the wonder grew,
That one small head could carry all he knew.

Oliver Goldsmith

Starting
at school

Packing the trunk

Curiously, the sensation itself, the approach of the day itself, has faded. . . . I see in my bedroom, for a week or so beforehand, that terrible play-box (how ironical a name!) of white wood, with – painted on it, plainly and immensely in black – as if it were tarred and feathered upon it – those impersonal initials F.O.S.S. I see the preparations, the fussy packing and consequent unpacking; I hear the worried, excited voices, rather pleased but argumentative, crying, 'I can't have forgotten the soap, can I? The only thing is to see. . . . We shall have to unpack again', or discussing the various essential items of clothing and impedimenta, figuring in the printed list issued by the authorities for the help of the parents, and classified in the cant terms of the school:

"'One pair of Black Oxford House Shoes (elastic-sided).' . . . Well, that's plain enough. . . . I'll just pop them in the box before we forget.

"'One pair best Bowling Trousers.' . . . Now what can they be? . . . I wish Mr Wolfe would be more explicit. . . . Perhaps it's these grey ones?

"'One Land-and-Water.' Oh dear, what can that be?

"'One strong Umbrella.' . . . That's simple enough.

"'One pair Association Football Boots (no steel caps).' . . . That's so that the boys shan't hurt one another.'

And so forth. . . . I see, too, the badges of my degradation, the hideous garb laid out; and the things intended to compensate one for it in the imagination, the supplies of oranges, biscuits, Suchard chocolate in slabs, – all, again, purchased strictly in accordance with rules laid down in the encyclical. . . . Then I remember nothing more, until the afternoon of the day itself, when a friend of my mother's gave me a piece of unconventional advice for which I have always been grateful to him. 'Don't believe what everyone tells you, that school is the happiest time of your life. Or you'll be miserable. It isn't. You'll hate every moment of it.'

Osbert Sitwell

Another new school

My mother said, 'You're going to school.' Now I had not been to school since leaving South Shields and I was not eager to return. All the same, she took me along to the Adelphi Terrace Public School, about half a mile from where we lived. When we got to the place I clung to the railings and refused to enter, yelling my head off. My mother was the stronger, and, after a struggle, I found myself before a large man who asked me several questions which I failed to understand. He had a pronounced Glasgow brogue, much too harsh for me. Besides, I was too shy to respond. Mother left me with a promise to return and, meanwhile, I was taken to a classroom and given a seat at a small desk. I was put into a class suited to my age, and I was acutely distressed when, along with other children, I was expected to answer questions on a subject about which I knew nothing. We were asked to write in an exercise book what we considered were suitable answers. What could I do? I did what I suppose was shameful. I tried several times to look over the shoulder of a boy in the desk below me. But it was no use; the teacher must have realised by my movements that something was wrong. A few days later, in a new and lower class, I gradually adapted myself to the situation. We were one day examined not by our own teacher but by a man whom the teacher introduced as the Visiting Inspector. He examined us in mental arithmetic and other subjects and I speedily responded. He was impressed and remarked, 'That boy has his head screwed on straight.' This is the sole commendation I ever received in my limited education.

Lord Shinwell

A Paulina's locker

I was appalled by my first day at school. There were hundreds and hundreds of girls (actually four hundred and sixty). Hordes of them flocking along those endless passages – and no male in sight except Ruthven, the hall porter, and Gustav Holst, the Director of Music.

There were great underground changing rooms, rows of livid varnished pinewood lockers like up-ended coffins in which hockey sticks, shoes, jerseys, combs and any accumulated personal belongings were thrust. Mine I tried and failed to keep in some kind of order. As I frequently lost or forgot the key which we were supposed to wear like dismal rosaries around our necks, I was in permanent trouble. And yet my locker felt the only part of the school that was really mine. Those early days I wanted to climb inside and hide there.

Diana Hopkinson

Maxie makes his point

W.M.G.* was showing two prospective parents round Windsor and I, as head of house, was roped in to accompany them. The wife, who gushed slightly, said, 'Of course, Mr Gordon, my son tells me everything.' Maxie replied, 'Well, all I can say, Madam, is that he is either a liar or a fool.'

The wife was rather put out, but the husband roared with laughter and the boy came to the school.

Alan Wright

*Walter Maxwell Gordon, headmaster of Wrekin College, 1920–44.

Not exactly uniform

I suppose like most little girls I was always impressed by the bright lights and lots of colours. Guess I haven't changed much. It didn't take long for me to realise that dancing meant you could wear some lovely and outrageous clothes and get away with it. But back at school we had to keep very much to our regulation uniforms. You know what I mean, gymslips and black shoes, and all that. Well as time went by we all learned the little dodges you could use to be able to sneak in little bits of style and fashion. I must say the day I first saw that bright flame-red, nylon frilly 'sticky-out' petticoat I was bowled over. I fell in love with it straight away. I had to have it. Before long, my mum gave in and bought it for me.

The next thing was to try to find a way to wear it to school. At first it just seemed impossible; there could be no way I could ever turn up without being far too obvious. Then I came up with the solution. I put the petticoat on underneath my gymslip and rolled it over and over at the waist until it was level with the bottom of my school uniform. Perfect, only my friends and me would know I was wearing it.

Off I went to school next day and soon became the talk of the class. Then we were called to assembly. Somehow I ended up in the front row directly in front of the Head and the other teachers. After a couple of minutes some mean person behind me quietly reached down and pulled the bottom of the slip down sharply. The gymslip shot up to my waist and the bright red petticoat sprang out like a ballet dress. There was no way I could save myself. The whole school burst out laughing until they noticed that the Head was 'not amused'.

I got a severe ticking-off and I felt so awful and embarrassed that I quietened down considerably after that. Well, for a few weeks, anyway!

Arlene Philips

Belt and braces

'Why have you such a slope-shouldered, belly-protuberant, stooping and deformed appearance? Answer me that, oh ye faithless and hunchbacked generation'.

The headmaster of my prep school looked very much like God. He had long, white, slightly curly hair, and was old and beautiful. He wore a dark suit which had shortish trousers showing the tops of his highly-polished black boots. He also spoke in God's prose, a mixture of the *Old Testament* and Rudyard Kipling's *Just So Stories*.

'Draw nigh and hearken to me, oh litter of runts and weaklings. I say unto you that you are round-shouldered through the wearing of braces! Unbutton your braces and cast them from you. Each boy to acquire a dark-blue elastic belt with a snake buckle, to be slotted neatly into the loops provided at the top of school shorts.'

'Dear Mummy,' I wrote, in the compulsory letter home, 'I don't like it here at all. I know it said braces on the clothes list, but we're not allowed braces any more. In fact we have to cast them from us. Noah told us this in assembly' (we were expected to call the staff by their nicknames; the headmaster's was 'Noah'). 'Could you send me a dark-blue belt with a snake buckle as quickly as you can?'

'What, gasping for breath, ye red-faced and pop-eyed generation?' Noah looked at us with amused contempt at the following week's assembly.

'Why do you show such clear signs of stomach contraction? Why are you an offence to the eye, all tied up like parcels? I say unto you, there will be no more belts or the wearing thereof. Abandon belts! Each boy to equip himself with a decent pair of sturdy elastic braces!'

'Dear Mummy,' I wrote, 'I still don't like it here. Would you please send me a new pair of braces as soon as you can? I cast mine aside and now I can't find them. And now I have to cast aside my belt . . .'

John Mortimer

First day memories

No-one told me about going to school.

I remember no warnings, no cushioning hints that freedom fell away from us at the age of five. One morning I simply woke up and found myself there, surrounded by faces I had never known, voices unfamiliar, shapes that made no sense.

What are the pieces that remain, still standing out in some sort of relief, their definition undimmed by the passing years which have gone out themselves like lights, one by one?

The smells.

The smells remain. Still sticking inside my skull, naked and sharp as electric bulbs, bringing into prominence the dusty old corridors and corners of the brain.

Always the smell of new varnish opens up these closed old cells, not dead as I imagined them to be, but still frighteningly jailored by the turnkeys of the present – the action of a pen upon blank paper, the saying of a name long unmentioned, the echoes stirring in an empty room.

Our desks had been varnished for the start of the new term, but nothing could conceal their dismal and dismaying oldness. Old oak they had been made from, older than Epp's coffin and Epp herself who had sat at them perhaps, these solid slabs of oakwood, brutally banged together to form mantraps for boys and girls, to keep us sitting in rows, two by two, like the animals in the ark; sealed in from the great flood of unknowing that raged around the edges of our lives.

So we sat there, heads upright, faces to the front, torsos and calves perpendicular with the walls, thighs aligned to the plane of the ceiling, feet flat on the floor, toes together. We sat thus, in the shapes of broken crosses, for the next seven years. We sat and sat – and grew into the angles of our desks, and the wood of the desks, dead coffinwood, grew into our souls.

On my first day I was beset by colonies of bigger boys and girls who preyed on me without mercy. I left my mother's hand and walked sullenly through the iron gates of the school. At once they zoomed in on me. Arms spread stiffly like wings, they swooped and soared, their goggle-eyes stabbing as they advanced, their clattering tongues machine-gunning me dead with fear before they closed. Dog-faced dog-fighters, gull-hungry for attack, they struck, tore, bit, clung. They swung from the twin ends of my long knitted scarf till my tongue turned black. They knocked me breathless to the hard ground. Their faces jostled in the sky like bunches of bruised fruits, and their busy hands rifled my pockets to take whatever could be found to be eaten. Then they were off and I was initiated.

Laurie Lee

Monogamy is when you have a broken stereo. Polygamy is when you have a parrot and its guts have come out.

Nuclear families use electricity from nuclear power stations.

All hopes dashed

I had won a place at the Portsmouth Southern Grammar School for Girls. My sisters justifiably accused me of being a 'Creep' as my image of being a pseudo beatnik rapidly changed to that of 'Little Miss Prim'. I no longer slopped around in drainpipe corduroys and striped T-shirts, affecting 'kiss curls' and bopping with the door handle as my partner to 'Cathy's Clown' and 'Jailhouse Rock'.

My deportment improved dramatically as I had visions of myself sporting the famous blue sash awarded to the best groomed girls at my new school. Auntie Joan, the resident hairdresser at Kassassin Street, made sure my hair was cut an inch above my starched white collar and a neat fringe ensured the clean cut image.

I became obsessed with the stationery department at W.H. Smith, examining HB and B pencils with great enthusiasm and preparing my uniform which consisted of a navy-blue gymslip, white shirt and dark blue tie. Only fawn socks and brown shoes were acceptable, and of course the regulation navy blue knickers. Every garment was dutifully lined with freshly printed name tags, including my new brown satchel which seemed enormous as the few new contents rattled round in it. I keenly modelled the new 'gear' for at least a month before the great day.

Breakfast was unthinkable that balmy September morning as I dressed for the main event. I was shining from top to toe. Pristine clean, I paced around our tiny house as I was ready far too early and succeeded in making everyone else as nervous as I was. Even though my sisters were pupils at the school there was an unwritten code that you did not acknowledge each other from the time you left the house so I walked to the bus stop alone, hoping all the neighbours were watching me.

The butterflies accelerated on seeing the No. 18 approaching. There was no turning back now. It was a great comfort to see Ann Prescott and Linda Morton on top of the bus; we all eyed each other, feeling very self conscious in our black Panama hats and not talking to each other.

However, a very different Marilyn Cole arrived home at 12 noon (I refused to stay to school dinner). Even though my nerves had been frayed earlier that morning I at least displayed a certain confidence which had totally disappeared on my return.

My deportment suffered as I clunked down the street with my heels hanging out of my new shoes which had rubbed big blisters; my winter uniform was far too hot and the worst blow of all was the fact I was to learn French instead of German. (My sisters were both in the German stream, so I had envisaged them helping me with my homework).

So there it was; all my hopes dashed in three hours. No German, no deportment sash and the dreaded Miss Hacking to contend with.

Marilyn Cole

. . . Hardy also wrote *Tess of the Dormobiles*

Another candidate referred to 'Jayne Austin's heroin'. *John Hollinshead*

Unwillingly to school, Aussie-style

If you think you have problems now with primary correspondence education, that's only the shower to toughen you up before the storm, and in some cases the cyclone, of secondary education.

Sammy and Melissa have finished Grade seven, so gird your loins, Mum and Dad. The first hurdle is the uniform. Sammy, with a carefree childhood behind him where only bare feet and elastic sides figure, has now to be introduced to shoes, and shoes all day and seven days a week. Mums who can put up with the whinging, buy a pair and make him wear them on Sunday afternoons during the holidays. When the whinging subsides a bit, tell him about ties, but leave the school to make him wear one. Melissa, in the meantime, has to know about gloves and school hats, and Melissa is going to whinge about four times as long as Sammy: there's nothing you can do about it, except make your mind a blank, and say 'yes dear,' at intervals, but be ready to pick up the changed note in the voice when she says 'you don't love me any more, do you?' so that you give the right answer.

Sammy started Grade one with his little black mate, Frankie, and has refused point-blank to go to boarding school unless Frankie goes too, on the grounds that mates have to share the bad times as well as the good. So you've done all the explaining to his parents, and applied for the grants, and organised the paperwork, and Frankie is going too. Frankie doesn't whinge: he gives you a big white-toothed grin, so maybe he'll help Sammy through.

He'll help him all right! It's three weeks after you've said goodbye to them at school eight hundred miles away, and here comes the mail-truck, and my god isn't that Sammy and Frankie sitting up on the load on the back! They're dirty, and their clothes are dirty, and they're barefooted, and they've walked and hitched rides until they met the mailman 200 miles back. It's not a fit place for a kid, Mum, the headmaster belted them. Why did the headmaster belt them? Well, they were starving, absolutely dying of starvation, and there was no bush tucker in the benighted place, but they were lucky enough to do what they'd often done out bush at home: they caught a cat. A big boy saw the fire they made, and pimped on them, and the headmaster belted hell out of them, and said some terrible things, and Frankie said why don't we go home.

Dad has a talk to them, and Dad drives them back, but Mum's job is the hardest. You try writing a letter to the headmaster apologising for your son and his mate eating the school cat!

Marie Mahood

First Day at Grammar School

Having passed my 11 plus I was tucking into my first Posh School Dinner. Actually, I'd just finished my rice pudding, when the teacher said 'Hands up anyone who hasn't had a sweet yet'. Gosh, I thought, all this and a *toffee* as well.

Up went my hand, along came more pudding which I promptly devoured. 'Anyone else not had a sweet?' My hand in the air. A third 'Pudding' arrived, which I started on, then a voice in my ear 'Is everything all right Bernard?' 'No Miss.' 'Why?' 'Well, they keep bringing me puddings when all I want is a sweet!!'

It took me a long time to live it down.

Bernie Clifton

Shoe bags

We had a marvellous group of dedicated spinster teachers, who all plaited their long hair in two ear muffs. Miss Platt, the formidable needlework teacher, informed us that our first project was to make our own shoe bags. They were simple, drawstring affairs in navy blue cotton with our names embroidered in white silk. She announced in a sincere tone, 'You will never get anywhere in life without a shoe bag.' I am delighted to say I now have Louis Vuitton shoe bags in my closet.

Marilyn Cole

Blue skirts into blue stockings or recollections of Christ's Hospital

Each new girl saw Miss Robertson alone, but she did not try to put me at my ease or even to welcome me, I don't know what she said to other girls. There was not even that presumption of family feeling which Mr Bowyer had thundered at Coleridge. The interview was used to ensure that I would know her as the figure of authority in the school. First she impressed on me that I ought to have a keen sense of gratitude and to try to give to the school as well as to take from it. I listened to this with proper attention as my mother had said very much the same to me at home. Then looking at me disapprovingly she said,

'I see that you have been to school before, Annie –', here I interrupted her, which I don't suppose improved her opinion of me.

'My name isn't Annie, it is Anne, but I am called Louie at home.'

'Very well child, we will call you Louie, but you must not interrupt and you must address me as Madam.'

'Yes, Madam.'

'I see that you have been to school before child, so you can tell me what is the worst thing any school girl can do.'

I was a bit staggered by this, but went ahead fairly confidently as I knew what my father considered the worst sin ever.

'Telling lies, Madam.' I said.

'That is certainly very wrong,' replied Miss Robertson, 'but it is not the worst thing a school girl can do.'

'Cheating, Madam.' I said again.

'No, Louie.'

'Stealing, Madam.'

'No, child.'

I couldn't think of anything else except murder and adultery, I did not think she could possibly mean the first and I did not know what the second one meant and was afraid she might ask me. If Ronald Searle had created St. Trinians before 1916 I might possibly have tried murder, but I doubt it.

'I don't know anything else,' I said at last.

'The worst thing a school girl can do.' announced Miss Robertson, solemnly, 'is to pass notes in class to another girl.' And with this pronouncement on school girl wickedness my interview with Miss Robertson ended.

Louie Angus

Eccentric teachers

Music lessons

At Lancing I started to compose songs and once again took piano lessons. One day in the practice room, the music master came in. 'What on earth are you playing?' he demanded. 'Something by Noel Coward, sir,' I replied. 'Noel who?' Then after a thoughtful pause, he said. 'Oh yes, that's the fellow who writes music with his tongue in someone else's cheek.'

Billy Milton

An eye for a flawless complexion

The Headmaster, always called 'the Chief' (or less amiably, 'the Chump') was not an accessible man. His well-trimmed beard, and his rather eerie method of progress, walking stiffly erect through classrooms and corridors in soundless sandshoes, looking neither to right nor left, led to his being identified with Jesus Christ. I think he was painfully shy. However, he was an excellent, if alarming, teacher of the Classics. 'Get it right, man! Get it right!' he would explode to girl and boy alike, tapping his rubber-soled shoe impatiently on the floor. Yet he conveyed to us his own genuine enthusiasm, for Greek in particular, and it was rumoured that his favourite girl of the moment used to be summoned to private Greek tuition, and have her hand squeezed under a rug. The whole school knew who was the Chief's reigning sultana at any one time. He had a connoisseur's eye for a flawless complexion and lovely, expressive eyes. I would hardly have dared to sum him up then, as I do now, as an old hypocrite and a far from admirable character.

Frances Partridge

Sikhs wear turbines.

Monogamy is love for friends or animals.
Polygamy is a love for your school.

Increase in the population is an advantage because more people die.

The way in which people were likened to sheep in Isaiah's prophecies was that they all wore sheepskins and had long hair.

Martin Luther King was a coloured man right from an early age.

Our church has tainted glass windows.   *Rev. H. W. White*

24

Absent-minded professor

There are several set pieces used to illustrate The Professor's absent-mindedness – the story that he made his way to Shrewsbury station, could not remember where he was going, and telephoned to his secretary to find out; or the story that (when headmaster of St. Bees) he went to the station to welcome a visitor, climbed into the train and disappeared, leaving his visitor to find his way to the school as best he could. It is recorded that, on one occasion while he was at Shrewsbury, he forgot his promise to preach a sermon elsewhere, and was heard talking on the telephone on the Sunday morning: 'Good gracious! What? Harvest Festival! Murder – it can't be true! Never mind, you must let me come and preach it next year!' But my recollections are chiefly of smaller incidents. To one of the twins Roualeyn and Francis Cumming-Bruce, he asked 'Are you you or your brother?'

Derek Hudson

An Edwardian childhood

Miss Weisse, the headmistress, had an original and bracing personality. She could not abide sentimentalism and sloppy schoolgirl friendships and infatuations.

'You remind me of a rancid pool of cod-liver oil,' she remarked to one poor girl who was indulging in a 'pash' for the music mistress. But she, too, seemed positively irritated when she learned that I had been victimised! She once told me how angry she was because I was not living 'up to the standards set by your grandmother', a remark which seemed strange to me, since she could not have known my grandmother.

But she did make one observation which remained in my mind. 'I hear people say that I am not fair,' she said once. 'I would like you to understand that I don't try to be fair. It is too difficult; and, besides, life isn't fair, but you have to put up with it.' All considered, this was not a bad guide line for the future.

Eva, Marchioness of Reading

His master's voice

A wealthy man, who was a keen shot, rented a shoot each year. As it was impossible for him to keep a gun dog he hired one from the gamekeeper. One year the keeper said that he had the finest gun dog he had ever known, a dog so talented that he called him 'The Master'.

At the end of the first day, having had the finest day's shooting in his life, the man agreed that 'The Master' thoroughly deserved his name, and there and then arranged to have the dog next year.

On arrival the following year he went straight to the keeper's cottage to collect the dog.

'Hello, sir,' said the keeper, 'I'd rather you had a different dog.'

'Why?' asked the man 'What's wrong with "The Master"?'

'Well,' said the keeper, 'he was so good I decided to call him "The Headmaster" and now he sits on his backside all day long doing absolutely nothing.'

R. Hart

Mad hatter's party

The two staffs of Shoreham and Hurstpierpoint used to meet together for a joint conference. The Reverend Frederick Mertens had no sense of taste or smell, and Pennell, one of the Hurst masters, was almost blind. Mertens was bending down low over his food to scrutinise it (his method of testing food owing to his defective sense of taste), and Pennell, dimly seeing Mertens' clerical collar almost on the table, mistook it for the rim of his teacup and proceeded to pour milk down Mertens' neck.

Historian of Hurstpierpoint

No, no, a thousand times no

S. P. B. Mais, the novelist, hit Sherborne like a whirlwind. Anything he taught became dramatic. In mathematics in the lower forms he awarded marks by the thousand. It caught the imagination of his pupils. They enjoyed announcing that as a result of the morning's work they had amassed 35,000 marks and the winner at the end of term proudly informed his parents that he had collected over ten million marks. The book-keeping of these arithmetic sums presented no problem for Mais; he knocked off the noughts and entered in his book Smith 35, James 33.

Evelyn Waugh

Identifying staff

Montague John Rendall who had been headmaster all the time that I was there (Winchester) . . . was shamelessly unconventional. On one occasion, when he wanted to interview a new cook, he arranged to meet her on the platform of Reading station. He travelled on the school train which was taking the boys back to London for the holidays. At Reading, we were astonished to see him get out and put a red flower in his mouth. It was the agreed method of identification, and in a few seconds, a buxom, middle-aged lady, with a red flower in *her* mouth, advanced towards him along the platform. As we did not know that she was a prospective cook, we were delighted by the whole episode.

Sir Kenneth Clark

Jason and the Juggernauts

Questions about the curriculum and discipline abound in education, but often it's the questions from the children which cause the most trouble.

Many children believe that a teacher is a multi-purpose hypermarket-cum-entertainment centre, running on solar energy, capable of instantly satisfying all requests ranging from:

'Mother I'm not going to school this morning.'
'Why not?'
'The boys don't like me and the staff don't like me.'
'Son you are going to school, you're forty-five years old and you're the Headmaster'

'Sir, have you got a valve for my BMX tyre?'
– through
'Sir, do you want a game of conkers?'
– to
'Sir, have you got a telephone directory for South Cardiff?'
All of these can be answered by the use of one very short word.

It would be nice to think that all questions sprang from a thirst for knowledge, from innocent and lively minds kindled by burning curiosity; undoubtedly children are interested in history –
'Sir, why did the Japanese bomb Poole Harbour?'
– in geography –
'Sir, which way is Mecca?'
and disadvantaged minorities –.
'Sir, why don't you get a decent car?'

Michael Edwards

On the move

Headmasters of private schools are divided into two classes: the workers and the runner-up-to London.

P. G. Wodehouse

Porter's Ploy

There was a comical science master called Dr Porter. He was an exhibitionist who loved to astonish his pupils. He was a confirmed and enthusiastic spiritualist and did not hesitate to preach spiritualism as the religion of the future to all his pupils. His religion took a peculiar and somewhat exhibitionist form. He brought one day into his division (at Eton) a little bomb. He explained to us that it was the most potent bomb in the world. If it should be dropped it would destroy all Eton. Then he dropped it on the floor and at once bade us fall on our knees and recite the Lord's Prayer. We did this and there was no explosion. 'God has stayed his hand,' he told us.

Christopher Hollis

The Head speaks:

'A parent once said to me that half the teachers here did all the work and the other half did nothing – I can assure you that the reverse is the case.'

Could do better

At an end-of-term staff meeting shortly after the Headmaster had checked all the reports for the customary mistakes – misspelt Christian names, inaccurate grammar and so forth – a Classics colleague, who was known for the brevity of his reports and who prided himself on his command of grammar and usage, smugly inquired of the Head if he had found any split infinitives in his reports. Without a moment's hesitation the head replied tartly 'It is very difficult to find a split infinitive in a two-word report, Mr Johnson.'

Suitably mortified, and following a Headmasterly edict the following term that all reports should be of at least two lines, Johnson wrote of one pupil:

Satis-
factory.

Anthony G. C. Brown

A whiff of stew

Miss Pride's Academy not only taught its post-war pupils embroidery and penmanship; it taught us the fine distinction between the acrid smell of wet knickers and the pervasive smell of wet cabbage. And just as the Jesuits capture your soul at the age of seven, so Miss Pride captured our nostrils at the more impressionable age of four.

Perhaps, today, I scent the whiff of overcooked cabbage more frequently than the tang of somewhat-stewed knicker. One's contemporaries are, despite urban pressures, less likely to release a flood of emotion when distressed. But when struck by either scent, a world more Dickensian than Dickens's swims reflexively to mind. A black-garbed grey-topped Miss Pride some ten feet tall laying a bamboo cane on the table for instant silence; cuddly Miss Priest remembering something about geography while fondling a decrepit dog with different coloured eyes; Billy Brennan elected Head Boy by the sycophantic class because he has the most sweet cigarettes. Little did you guess, Miss Pride, that decades after your death you would live on in my nostrils.

Colin Walsh

A dame-school of the twenties

In 1922, at the age of six, I was sent to my first school. I remember the year because the first task the new pupils were set was to write the date on their slates. I was impressed: 1922 seemed to be entirely new; up to that time I had probably believed that it would always be 1921.

The school, which consisted of about a dozen girls and boys, all of whom I knew well, was run by two elderly ladies, Miss W. and Miss J., who had indeed been responsible for introducing the children of the neighbourhood to schooling for more than twenty years.

Miss W. was a masterful little woman with a very straight back; she invariably wore a black-and-grey flannel blouse, with long buttoned sleeves and a little edging of net at the neck, and a straight black serge skirt to her heels. Miss J., on the contrary, was a plump, motherly body whose chief physical characteristic was a mole on her cheek from which protruded, like pins on a pincushion, a number of stiff little hairs; she smelt of strong tea and was in loving charge of the smallest pupils.

The school day began with a hymn, chosen by each pupil in turn: *Onward Christian Soldiers* was the favourite and was eventually banned as being too popular. The school then divided into two classes, Miss W. being in kindly but very firm charge of the eight- and nine-year-olds. The curriculum was extensive: even the youngest learnt Latin and French (taught by an elderly expatriate who wept when we were called upon to shrill the *Marseillaise*), besides the usual English and mathematical subjects. At the end of the afternoon we were assembled in the Schoolroom – the front parlour of one of a row of terraced cottages – to sing *God Save the King,* Miss W. playing the accompaniment while standing bolt upright at the piano.

The accent, indeed, was strongly on the Church of England and patriotism. On Empire Day we were made to march past a Union Jack stuck on a pole in the centre of the playground, saluting as we passed it. On one occasion a boy named Robert (he was normally known as Billy but we were all addressed by the formal version of our names; my brother Dick was called Roland because there was already a Richard) committed the truly awful offence of cocking a snook at The Flag instead of raising his palm smartly to his brow as he had been taught.

For this crime, Robert was sentenced to stand on a bench in front of 'the whole school' with a sheet over his head. During a momentary absence of Miss W. he contrived to work his head through an enlarged hole in the sheet and performed a bat-like dance up and down the bench. The rest of us, who up to then had been appalled by the hideous nature of what he had done, and impressed by the nature of his punishment, were now unable to restrain our laughter. Miss W., returning at speed like a small black fury, actually dragged Robert from the bench and ordered him to return home at once, accompanied by a stiff note to his parents.

Punishments of this kind (including in the case of girls being undressed and put to bed in Miss W.'s bed) were not uncommon, but we had our festivities as well, including the summer picnic when we played games on the slope of a neighbouring hill, and the Christmas Party, when Miss W. and Miss J., who owing to the extreme modesty of their fees had very little to spare on frills, contrived to decorate the Schoolroom with homemade paper garlands (we helped to make them in the Art Class), to provide lemonade and buns, and to organise an endless round of games and competitions in which all, winners and losers alike, were rewarded with pear-drops.

On one such occasion, however, the inventiveness of Miss W. went a sad step too far. We were received at the door by Miss J. and there was no sign of the senior teacher as we entered the decorated Schoolroom, in one corner of which was a large and ungainly heap of spangled cotton-wool. When all were assembled, Miss J. announced that the Christmas Fairy was about to pay us a visit. And she did. The heap of cotton-wool heaved asunder, and out sprang the Christmas Fairy, complete with wand, starred headband, white muslin skirt reaching to the ground, and pince-nez on a chain.

There was an instant of uncertainty, and then pandemonium.

The smaller children shrieked with terror, the elder ones yelled with laughter. Above the uproar could be heard the voice of Miss J. – 'It's all right, dears, it's only Miss W.,' – and of Miss W. herself – 'Quiet, children, I am entertaining you.'

That was an unforgettable occasion. Equally so, in a quite different way, was the last time I saw Miss W. It was some twenty-five years later, and I took my four-year-old daughter to see the now very old but still very upright lady. The cottage was no longer a school; the Schoolroom had been transformed into a typical late-Victorian parlour. Miss J. was out shopping; there was a powerful smell of tea in the air.

Miss W. and I talked of old days and of the pupils whose photographs, framed in passe-partout, stood and hung everywhere. Robert had been killed in the war: 'I liked that boy,' said Miss W. firmly, 'he had *character*.'

As we walked away down the well-remembered playground I said to my daughter, who had sat speechless with boredom throughout the interview 'That old lady taught us.'

'What old lady tortoise?' she asked with sudden interest.

P. Tewson

Summerhill – the progressive school

Once a woman brought her child of seven to see me. 'Mr Neill,' she said, 'I have read every line you have written; and even before Daphne was born, I had decided to bring her up exactly along your lines.'

I glanced at Daphne who was standing on my grand piano with her heavy shoes on. She made a leap for the sofa and nearly went through the springs.

'You see how natural she is,' said the mother. 'The Neillian child.' I fear that I blushed.

A. S. Neill

Teacher (pointing to 'I have went' on blackboard): 'Now, why is that sentence wrong?'
Boy: 'Because you 'aven't went yet – you're still here.'

Teacher: 'Now, Tommy, what's a niche in a church?'
Boy: 'Same as anywhere else – only you mustn't scratch it!'

Donald McGill

God Bless the Prince of Wales

Our headmistress might have been made of parchment. She had a yellow powdered face and flat paper-sculptured hair. She wore beige, and walked stiff-necked and stiff-kneed with her feet pointing sideways in toffee-coloured shiny shoes. The kids called her old Ma Pegtop. Sometimes she smiled at a pretty or nicely-dressed little girl, but her obsession was with royalty. Her desk was in the corner of the hall and was partially screened from the draughty doors by four hinged pieces of polished wood. This was plastered with newspaper cuttings and photographs of King George, Queen Mary and old Pegtop's favourite, the Prince of Wales. We marched into the hall for prayers to the thump of the piano and stood for the whole time. We whined through the hymn, picking up the words and tunes of *All Things Bright and Beautiful* and *Fight the Good Fight* on alternate days, and then gasped through The Lord's Prayer with hands together and eyes closed. A resounding smack punctuated the prayer every so often as a teacher crept along the lines and slapped the back of a boy's head who was caught peeping through his fingers.

After prayers we had a bulletin on the health and activities of the Royal Family.

Rose Gamble

A sensitive beak

I cannot remember all the other thousands of splendid things that old Corkers cooked up to keep his class happy, but there was one that I shall never forget which was repeated at intervals of about three weeks throughout each term. He would be talking to us about this or that when suddenly he would stop in mid-sentence and a look of intense pain would cloud his ancient countenance. Then his head would come up and his great nose would sniff the air and he would cry aloud, 'By God this is too much. This is going too far. This is intolerable.'

We knew exactly what was coming next, but we always played along with him. 'What's the matter, Sir? What's happened? Are you alright, Sir? Are you feeling ill?'

Up went the great nose again, and the head would move slowly from side to side and the nose would sniff the air delicately as though searching for a

---

Once in a blue moon a child asks a question to which the answer is blatantly obvious:

'Sir, why don't you give up teaching and go and do something exciting like being a mercenary?'

'But I am one.'

leak of gas or the smell of something burning. 'This is not to be tolerated' he would cry. 'This is unbearable.' 'But what's the matter, Sir?' 'I'll tell you what's the matter,' Corkers would shout. 'Somebody's farted!'

'Oh no, Sir' 'Not me, Sir' . . . 'Not me, Sir' . . . 'Its none of us, Sir.'

At this point, he would rise majestically to his feet and call out at the top of his voice, 'Use door as fan! Open all windows!' This was the signal for frantic activity and everyone in the class would leap to his feet. It was a well rehearsed operation and each of us knew exactly what he had to do. Four boys would man the door and begin swinging it back and forth at great speed. The rest would start clambering about on the gigantic windows which occupied one whole wall of the room, flinging the lower ones open, using a long pole with a hook on the end to open the top ones, and leaning out to gulp the fresh air in mock distress. While this was going on, Corkers himself would march serenely out of the room, muttering, 'It's the cabbage that does it. All they give you is disgusting cabbage and Brussel sprouts and you go off like fire-crackers.' And that was the last we would see of Corkers for the day.

Roald Dahl

Ongo Bongo

One of our temporary teachers in war-time was an elderly but vigorous man who taught geography. He suffered from an affliction which made his hand tremble – and his voice vibrated, too, though it was very powerful. One day he was, with difficulty, drawing a map of Africa on the blackboard, and when he reached the Congo he announced the name to his pupils, still with his back towards them.

Simultaneously, with no reference at all to the Congo, someone caused laughter in the class. The teacher swung round furiously, his ample white hair seeming to arrive a second later than the rest of him, and roared, *fortissimo tremulo*, 'I know, I know! Ongo Bongo, King of the Congo – we want none of your filthy rhymes here!'

None of us had the faintest idea what he was talking about. Alas that knowledge possessed by the teacher should be denied to his pupils!

Alan Wilkinson

Whose life?

At one period in the 60s I was a director of 'This is your life' when it was with the BBC. We decided to do a 'Goodbye, Mr Chips' story and to this end we fixed on a charming, erudite master well known in classic and cultural circles.

He was appropriately known as Mr 'Chips' Channon and was about to retire from his lifelong work at a fine public school in Taunton. We learned that at the coming retirement ceremony he would be presented with a farewell gift and the boys en masse would sing the school song – a suitable moment for Eamonn Andrews to step into view and say 'Schoolmaster Extraordinary, Chips Channon, This is your life'.

Now we knew that, as this was a big school and Mr Channon was a keen T.V. watcher, the merest glimpse of Eamonn would give the game away and result in the show being cancelled. Elaborate precautions were therefore required.

Eamonn arrived by helicopter and was dropped in a remote muddy field. From here he was whisked to the school in a saloon car with the windows dirtied over. At the school he was smuggled, disguised, into a subterranean passage that led to the school hall. In those days the show was live, so an air of high excitement and cloak-and-dagger prevailed. Finally the great moment came; the boys were singing, there was applause – and suddenly as if from nowhere Eamonn materialised and handed the Big Red Book to the subject. The school was electrified. The rest of the show went without a hitch and was a great success. After the end titles had rolled up the screen and we were off the air I went up on to the platform to ask the man of the hour how he'd enjoyed having his life story told.

His words showed clearly that a lot of our security had not been necessary. 'Chips' was indeed a viewer of T.V. but apparently he only watched if there was an art or music programme on. For in answer to my query he said, yes, he'd enjoyed the experience very much but who was that nice young Irish boy he'd been talking to?

Verre Lorrimer

A physics lesson

My housemaster at Bromsgrove was a stern man who demanded a healthy respect. His name was 'Freddie' Wallace-Hadrill. He was of medium height, sharp-featured, and the top of his head, which was almost flat, was thinly thatched. He was dark and he brushed his hair straight across his high forehead from east to west. His eyes were also dark and deep-set, and I believe he was blind in one of them – the result of an accident on a tennis-court, we always understood. He was a neat and tidy man who, sartorially, turned himself out, if not with the elegance of the Savile Row trendies, always with dignity and correctness. His suits were invariably of plain grey flannel and all included a waistcoat. The latter he wore throughout every season of the year and in all weathers. In midsummer the boys were frequently told that they could remove their jackets in class; rarely, however, or perhaps it would be fairer to say, with reluctance, in Freddie's classes, and it was at this time that his waistcoat came under discussion.

'Look at me,' he would say. 'I'm wearing a waistcoat. Do you know why I'm wearing a waistcoat, Carmichael?'

'Yes, sir. You're wearing it to keep the heat *out*.'

'Correct' – and as head physics master it was difficult to argue with him.

Ian Carmichael

Undermining the morale

I stood inside the headmaster's office like a (guilty) miscreant. His face was as solemn as an executioner's – I had been summoned obviously to be strongly reprimanded. 'Sit down, Abse,' he said, gathering about him his long black gown. He seemed to be a worried man. Of course it was wartime and he had especial administrative problems. Recently, not only had most of the lay staff been called up but Brother Bonaventure, our excellent history teacher, had left the school having volunteered to become a bomber pilot.

'Last Friday evening,' Brother Michael said in his Irish brogue, 'you gave a talk to the Sixth Form Society, did you not now?'

'Yes, sir,' I said, puzzled. 'It was a debate actually.'

'The subject of your talk was "The Bankruptcy of Marriage" am I entirely right?'

'Well, Brother . . .' I began.

Abruptly he lost control and shouted, 'I don't want you talking about that sort of t'ing to the boys at all. Not in this school. It's a good Cat'olic school and I won't have you undermining the morale of the others. One of the boys, offended, reported to me your desperate opinions and . . .'

'But Brother Michael, I . . .'

'*Quiet,*' he yelled.

I was amazed. There had been a debate the previous Friday evening and I had advocated that Marriage was an unnecessary institution. True, only one boy had voted for me – and he had been a Protestant – but surely nobody would have been offended enough to complain to the headmaster? I could hardly credit Brother Michael's own apparent disgust and anger. However, he now once more controlled himself. He sighed, pushed his rimless spectacles higher up the bridge of his nose and continued more reasonably, 'Now, Abse, sure, I know you would say nothing pornographic at all. I mean you do not have a dirty mind – unlike some of the other boys I could mention – but I will not have you –' and at this point his face suddenly suffused with blood and his voice grew dominantly loud, '– present a PERVERTED CREDO ABOUT MARRIAGE – do you understand?'

Dannie Abse

Dogged fury

The dottiest beak at my school was probably the myopic Colonel Smart, who tried to teach me French. I don't think he remembered much of the language. He was also a housemaster: it must have been an odd establishment. One day, on our way to the Colonel's hash-room (school-room), we encountered a large and amiable mongrel dog. We took this in with us, and it sat quietly at the back. When irate, which was often, it was Colonel Smart's habit to order the object of his wrath – frequently a random choice – to stand up on his bench. When order broke down completely, by no means rare, he would order everyone to stand on their benches. It so happened on this occasion. As we clambered up, the Colonel pointed at our canine friend 'And you, too', he shouted.

John Doxat

The Queen's carpet that never was

The news spread like lightning, especially in a small town like Khemisset: the town is at last to play host to an august royal guest, not Moroccan but British. The Queen of Great Britain, HM Queen Elizabeth II is scheduled to visit The Save The Children Fund School for Handicapped Children in Khemisset. A great honour for both the school and the town.

A metamorphosis is to be witnessed in Khemisset, usually a service station for travellers going to or from North to South Morocco. Khemisset has nothing to offer historically or touristically to persuade a royal guest to visit it, except that the town happens to include The Save The Children Fund School. It would not be exaggerating to say that The Save The Children Fund School has more or less put the town of Khemisset on the map.

The news about the Queen's visit circulated throughout the town. Inside the school itself there is a feeling of buzzing activity and excitement, everyone is thrilled at the prospect of meeting the Queen and the Duke of Edinburgh. Arrangements for the welcoming ceremony are well under way, children and staff alike all contributing to the preparations.

Local authority officials, at their forefront the Governor of the Province, paid many visits to the school. They offered to do all the decorating inside and outside the school, an offer which was greatly welcomed by the school staff. The school buildings were all whitewashed, roads freshly cemented, extra wheelchair ramps built, classroom desks substituted with brand-new ones, portraits of the Queen of Great Britain and King of Morocco were supplied in abundance. Banners welcoming the Queen and the Duke were displayed in numerous places. Tents were erected along the royal route from the town to the school, a stretch of three miles. All the preparations were going to plan. Work was carried out day and night, especially since the visit was announced at short notice. Everyone was looking forward to the big day.

However, the local authority officials wanted to lay down a carpet for the Queen and her entourage from outside the school and throughout the itinerary inside the school. At this stage some trouble started to emerge. The Headmaster categorically refused this offer, arguing that carpets are not laid down every day in the school compound; the Queen wants to see for herself the daily life routine of the school, so no carpets.

The province officials, including the Governor, could not accept this idea and insisted that carpets should be laid down for the Queen and Duke. Talks between both sides went on for quite a time but to no avail to start with. After another series of deliberations both parties reached a compromise: the Headmaster agreed to the laying of the carpets outside the school only, and the inside of the school should be left without carpets. This agreement was welcomed by both the Headmaster and the province officials. Preparations went ahead.

However, the Headmaster was still not quite at ease about the carpets and several times on the eve of the royal visit he commuted from his room to the school main gate to make sure that no carpet was laid down inside the school at the last minute. Luckily, no carpet was to be seen.

The next morning, the big day, children and staff woke up earlier than normal to get ready for the arrival. Outside the school dancers, musical bands and a huge excited crowd of nearby villagers were singing, dancing and shouting welcoming slogans. Everything was ready to meet the royal guests. The royal motorcade arrived to a rapturous welcome. Children were thrilled to meet the Queen and her entourage. The royal couple toured the school's carpetless ground like anyone else, to the great satisfaction of the Headmaster.

Driss Mekkaoui*

Finger Flicking good

When you're a kid, because you've had little or no chance to travel around and compare your experiences with other kids outside your immediate circle of playmates and school-friends, you tend to assume that everybody else's lives and habits are identical to your own. If there are a dozen kids out of twenty in your class who all breed rattlesnakes for pets and come to school on white rhinos you just naturally assume that's about the national average. Nobody ever tells you you're in a nuthouse.

Well it was the same for me with Finger Flicking. I just assumed that that was what everybody else was doing all over the world or, certainly, all over the British Isles.

Major Wormwell was the headmaster of this very wee little school that my mum and dad decided to pack me off to as soon as I was big enough to see over a desk and sit on a lavatory without a serious risk of drowning. And it was on that first day at school that the Major initiated me in Finger Flicking. He announced something like: 'As this is the first day of term you can all have this afternoon off.' All the six and seven year olds all round me started waving their arms in the air like helicopters. Even the Major joined in. Apparently it was what you did at school when you were pleased about something. To define it more precisely, you touch the thumb and middle finger of each hand together, and then, with the rest of your fingers splayed open and your elbows bent so that your hands are about level with your shoulders, you wave your hands back and forth from the wrist as fast as possible. The noise when done by a whole school of children at morning assembly can be deafening, but at my nice little school it happened a lot. Sometimes if the news just brought delight to one individual, he would stand

---

Driss Mekkaoui is himself a former pupil of this Save The Children Fund school. Born in Morocco, he contracted polio at the age of four, and has spent most of his life with the fund, although he completed his higher education in England at the universities of Bath and Sussex, and is now with the BBC Monitoring Service.

there happily flicking away all on his own. No embarrassment whatsoever. It was just what you did.

'Well done, Tarrant, you're only just nine and you've got all three letters right in "CAT". 'Thank you, Sir.' Flick, flick, flick. We all did it at the slightest hint of happiness. Indeed until I was twelve I flicked two or three times a week, sometimes on my own, sometimes with just a couple of close friends, sometimes with the whole school and the headmaster. Naturally I assumed that this was going on all over British classrooms at the same time. I mean I didn't know Major Wormwell was completely out of his mind, did I?

So when at the age of twelve I finally moved on to the big school I was in for a series of shocks. The first one was that I was no longer the most important boy in the whole wide world, head and captain of absolutely everything. I was an insignificant little worm. And if I ever forgot it, regular reminders were handed out by much bigger boys in the form of fairly savage beatings.

Another shock lesson I remember learning quite vividly on the first Monday morning assembly at my new school. The term had been in progress for less than a week, but over the weekend apparently our Ist XV rugby team had stuffed it up some other little bunch of 'Hooray Henries' by about sixty points to nil and the headmaster was absolutely delighted. 'A marvellous start', he told the whole school, 'a result we can all be justly proud of' (the fact that the Ist XV wouldn't get a single 'A' level between them and only one of them could do joined-up writing was not thought to be important). It was a great moment for all boys to share in, he told us, 'well done, School'. Well, I was absolutely delighted for my new-found colleagues and started waving my little arms and flicking my fingers like there was no tomorrow. Whirr . . . whirr . . . whirr. Flick, flick, flick, I went, along with all other eight hundred happy boys at my new school . . . , only after about thirty seconds I realized that the others weren't all doing it, in fact none of them was. Counting masters as well there were one thousand six hundred and thirty eight eyes all trained on this odd little fair-haired kid in the first form who had something seriously wrong with the ends of his fingers.

Only as I was being dragged out of my place by my ears and dumped outside the headmaster's study to await his displeasure (which turned out to be six very crisp ones across the backside for being a disruptive influence), only at that moment did I comprehend how unique had been Major Wormwell's way of expressing true happiness.

Chris Tarrant

A history teacher, who gives such entertaining lessons that even tough truants attend regularly, is reputed to end her lessons like this, 'Will Napoleon manage to get back to France? If he does will he get men to follow him? How will England's Iron Duke react? Be here, next week, same time, same place, to find out what happens next!'

Up in smoke

One day at Bolton County Grammar School, we were all crammed into our tiny lecture theatre for a talk from a visiting deep sea diver, who demonstrated his 'hard hat' and breathing apparatus, all pretty exciting stuff in those days before television.

He showed us a stick of gelignite which would detonate if dropped on the floor or tapped with a hammer and actually walked forward so that those on the front row could see it at close quarters. Then he placed it carefully on the desk and moved towards the blackboard, but suddenly he had lost our attention . . . for in stark horror, the packed audience sat galvanised as we watched the gelignite stick roll slowly to the edge of the desk . . . and drop to the floor.

One by one, our heads popped back into view to see the diver giggling merrily as he picked up the 'dummy' gelignite stick.

Of course, I remember my school mates and I all discussing, wouldn't it have been marvellous if we hadn't been there, but it had been real gelignite and our school had gone up in the air and spread itself in an even layer all over Bolton.

Johnny Ball

Whacker Paine

One of the features of a boys' boarding school during World War II was, of course, the absence of young masters – they nearly had all volunteered to go off and fight. Their places were taken by old men recalled to teaching from country cottages, the Albany or the sanatorium – most of them had scholarship and culture to impart, hardly any of them had retained their faculties and few of them could keep order in the classroom.

One such restored relic was Whacker Paine. He had nervously fought as a cavalry officer in the Boer War. His original teaching career had terminated suddenly in the early thirties after unwisely reviewing the school cadet force from his horse. A boy whom he had caned with venom that morning (the punishment was always preceded by the tiresome comment 'You are about to feel Paine') took his revenge from a hidden position in the chapel vaults and fired an air pistol from close range into the horse's flank as the parade went by. The band concealed the sound of the shot – Paine was badly thrown and he forthwith retired.

His success as a recalled wartime teacher was pitifully limited. Boys are merciless when given the opportunity to destroy the morale of a bad disciplinarian even though it hurts their conscience at the time.

One boy, McCaffertey, who was soon to be decorated for bravery on the Normandy beaches, led the baiting in the 'Military' Sixth. An air pistol was again part of the story. Paine foolishly read out in class the end of term reports he intended to write on each pupil. For McCaffertey, against whose sallies he was defenceless in the classroom, he read out as damning a report as could only have been inspired by a term of complete despair.

McCaffertey, meanwhile, as usual was not attending, he and his bosom friend were sitting in their accustomed places on the far side of the classroom (evacuation seldom provided teaching accommodation of orthodox shape) and they were taking it in turns with an air pistol to shoot at the stick of chalk which Whacker would invitingly stand on its end on the edge of the table. The sequence was well rehearsed. At a signal Paine's attention would be distracted to the other side of the room, a heavy book would be thrown to the floor boards and McCaffertey would fire at the chalk.

McCaffertey did not hear the reading of his end of term report; he was aiming carefully at his target, waiting for the noise of the book being pushed off the desk. Whacker Paine read out the vitriolic report, swung round on McCaffertey in triumph and looked into the muzzle of the gun. 'Don't shoot McCaffertey', he begged, 'Don't shoot, I'll alter it. I'll write anything you say.'

Rodney Exton

41

Ham and Humphrey

I don't think there was anyone in the entire school, from the tiniest new boy in IIb to the toughest blue-jowled First Fifteen thug, who wasn't a little afraid of Ham. He was one of three lay masters, the others all being monks (not that some of them weren't capable of producing instant silence when they entered a classroom, either). Mr Derham taught (naturally) maths (who ever heard of a frightening French or music teacher?). Even in those days he seemed a carry-over from a world of stern Victorian disciplines. It was rumoured that he had taught at the much smaller school which stood on the site before the monks came back from France in 1903 and merged with it. He had a tremendously scrubbed, neat, fastidious appearance with his bald top, white tonsure, white moustache, rounded stiff collar, and small neat body; an air of having come from some strict training college, turning out teachers in a hierarchy where any slovenliness was lower-class, belonging to a world where shapeless women wore men's caps back to front and nobody could think straight or logically.

He articulated with amazing clearness, as though he were Irving reaching the gallery. And indeed, like all good teachers, he was a compelling actor. 'You FOOLS!', he would rasp, 'you see a booby-trap, and you make a DIVE into it,' suiting the action to the word, hands extended over his head, leaping nimbly from his dais. He would cover the blackboard rapidly with figures, saying sometimes quite incomprehensible things such as 'So, we will do this by alternando and dividendo.'

There was a rather serious boy in my form called Humphrey. He came from North Wales. One day Ham turned from the board with some equation or other and said 'Let us see if THAT has penetrated any of your limited intelligences.' (Pause). 'You, Humphries.'

Humphrey took not the slightest notice, remaining bent over his exercise book.

'YOU, Humphries. I am speaking to YOU.'

Still Humphrey made no response. There was an awful silence as Ham walked down to his desk. We thought he was going to pull his ears off.

'HUMPHRIES!'

At last he looked up. He looked Ham straight in the eye and said quietly, respectfully, 'My name is Humphrey, Sir.'

In the total silence Ham went back to the board without a word and continued the class exactly as if nothing had happened. But we all knew something had.

Paul Jennings

Performing
pupils

Unaccustomed as I am

I was never really unhappy at Harrow. I mildly enjoyed my first terms at The Knoll, and greatly enjoyed my last terms. Even the house bully was quite genial to me. I was classified as 'mad' but also as an amusing 'madder'. My role was more or less the Harrow equivalent of court jester, a fact to which I owe an unusual introduction to public speaking. The Captain of the House XI invited me to attend his 'leaving supper', a great compliment, for such invitations were normally reserved for the élite of the house.

'I've asked *you*,' he said, 'because I want you to make a speech, and if you don't make us laugh, you're for it.'

This was by no means an idle threat. If my speech had been a failure I should have probably have been beaten.

I did not enjoy the supper, for my presence lowered the social tone of the party, and those who had only just scraped an invitation resented the fact that I had been included among the guests. Nobody addressed a word to me. My host, when he invited me to speak, added, 'Remember what I told you.' Fortunately my first feeble joke was a success, and I was given to understand that I had earned my supper. Thereafter public speaking never had any terrors for me.

Sir Arnold Lunn

Dance of the daisy keys

When I was very young my parents, doubtless to keep me quiet, gave me a typewriter. It was called the Simplex – very aptly, since the 'keys' were much like a dialling telephone. You picked your letter, dialled it to the central position, pressed down hard, and so, very laboriously, you were able to build up the imprint of a word, even a whole sentence, on a sheet of typing paper. It was with this machine that I set out at the age of about eleven to create not an article, or even a mini-story, but a complete school magazine. It took me the whole of one term to issue that single irreplaceable copy. And when it was done, the headmaster and his partners decided they could do better, and thereafter each term a school magazine was produced on a proper printing press.

I still have the 'Simplex' typewriter, but not alas that single irreplaceable copy. The 'Simplex' printing idea is now, of course, the daisy wheel used in so many electric typing machines and word processor printers.

I had made the mistake of revealing all about what went on amongst us when the previous headmaster's back was turned – the trench warfare with bricks and stones for grenades, the Red Indian wars with wooden maces built like mallets under the expert eye of the carpentry instructor, and bows and arrows constructed from the bamboos that grew around the lake. These bows were quite lethal, their range half the length of a football pitch, the arrows sharpened to a razor point or tipped with steel pen nibs (how the big ones made the small ones dance!).

44

Much later I donated this epic of prose and printing to the school for reproduction in the newer magazine. Alas, it was censored – it might upset the cheque-signing equilibrium of parents or even frighten prospectives away. But it was fun writing (not typing!) that little magazine, even more fun getting up to all that mayhem wot we shouldn't 'ave.

Hammond Innes

Are you still there?

At my grammar school I and the rest of my class of silly adolescent girls had the bright idea of locking me in the cupboard during an English literature lesson and hiding the key.

Ghostly rapping noises were heard, to the consternation of the teacher. We all thought it highly amusing at the time but it doesn't seem so funny to me now.

Glenda Jackson

Backward in coming forward

On my first day at school – Cavendish Road School, Balham – I ran away and hid under a newspaper hoarding at the local sweetshop thinking no-one would find me. My reticent nature dates from that time.

Jimmy Hill

Front row

At my boy's boarding school in Surrey, they decided to stage Gilbert and Sullivan's *Pirates of Penzance*. There were no girls to play in the chorus line. As I was one of the younger boys I was given the role of a girl dancer and my mother made me a beautiful costume complete with bonnet and dorothy bag. Thanks to my school, therefore, I can truthfully say I began life in the chorus.

David Hamilton

Cheaper by the dozen

When I was at boarding school I had a lot of trouble with my handwriting. It occurred to me that I might solve the problem if I had a typewriter. Accordingly, I wrote to the Good Companion Typewriter Co. in Leicester, and asked them to send me particulars of the models available and the prices.

There was no reply. But some weeks later, when I was sitting at my desk in the maths class, a boy appeared and whispered something to Mr Hobson, the maths master. Mr Hobson beckoned me forward and told me to go to the headmaster's office. When I got there, the headmaster questioned me about my letter. It transpired that the typewriter company had got the impression that the school itself was interested in buying typewriters in quantity and they had sent a large van-load of all their models; it was standing outside the window.

I was interested in flying at the time; I often wonder what might have happened if I had written to the Handley-Page Aeroplane Company?

Peter Jones

Useful stuff

Aged 5ish . . . Convent of the Sacred Heart, Forest Hill London.

About a week after starting school, the mother superior called at my home very worried about little Pat 'There seems something horribly wrong with her eyes'. Denials by both parents – but little Pat showed them (after much persuasion) what she had been doing durring prayer sessions . . . . She had learned to 'go cross eyed' (with absolutely no realisation that it showed).

Pat Coombs

Making good

My mother once suggested I should write and draw a strip cartoon based on my childhood and called 'Robert Rascal Schoolboy Racketeer'.

I suppose I was a rather mercenary youth, intent on doubling my pocket money by relieving other boys of theirs. My 'School Magazine', for instance, was nothing but crudely assembled jokes, caricatures of our teachers, *Beano*-style comic strips and news reports about what I was offering for sale.

It was reproduced on a jelly pad and sold for tuppence, high finance in 1938. That enterprise ended when my father noticed that my 'For Sale' column listed six of his favourite gramophone records and the family cat ('only five shillings with flea collar!')

I made very unstable fireworks in our garden shed and undersold Brocks while still harvesting some fine profits – but the business blew up on me.

From a billowing black cloud I emerged from the shed minus eyebrows and my customers lost confidence in my product. I bought and sold anything that interested boys – conkers, 3-speed gears for bikes, pen knives, glamour stills of Betty Grable, marbles, secret swearwords (in sealed envelopes), Sexton Blake paperbacks, frogs, torches, fountain pens, cap pistols and gob-stoppers. I vaguely recall a few shady sidelines too . . . 'Want to buy the answers to tomorrow's exam?'

Could I have grown up to be a merchant prince, a captain of industry? I doubt it. I was probably headed for nothing grander than a market stall. But thanks be to providence, I stumbled upon the easiest racket of them all. At age 16 I discovered that people would buy something from me that they couldn't take away and that I could keep. And I've been telling them the same sort of jokes ever since.

Bob Monkhouse

Smile, please

I can remember being called to the headmistress's office at ballet school and she said, 'Una we are going to expel you unless you stop this incessant giggling. It's the giggling that makes you so fat! And remember we don't usually take on children from local secondary schools'.

I did cut down on my giggling but took it up again as soon as I left school and have kept on ever since.

Una Stubbs

48

All aboard!

I went to Haileybury and Imperial Service Junior School at Clewer Manor near Windsor. I went there when I was seven years old. When I was eight, two friends of a similar age, whose names I believe were Perry and Low, and I decided it would be exciting to visit America.

Perry's father had something to do with the Cunard Line, so we decided to go to my house at Bray, collect a canvas canoe that I had, and paddle up the Thames, round the coast and catch the New York boat from Southampton. It all sounds pretty far fetched now, but when you are only eight years old the obstacles appear easily surmountable!

It was about five miles from Clewer Manor to my house, The Long White Cloud at Bray, and I remember during our runaway period, we heard dogs in the distance and thought they had got bloodhounds out after us.

When we got to my house, I can remember running across the lawn, from tree to tree, as we tried to get to the boat house to rescue the canvas canoe. Unfortunately, or should I say fortunately, my mother spotted us and called out, 'Stirling is that you?' We had been caught red-handed and, therefore, had to own up.

When we got back to school, the headmaster decided to punish us in the most drastic fashion. He cancelled a school outing the following day, not just for us three offenders, but for the entire school! We therefore had the full fury of the other sixty or seventy boys launched against us and they subsequently refused to speak to us for quite a long time! It was a pretty harsh punishment, and rather unfair on the others, but it certainly cured any ideas of anyone trying to get to America.

Stirling Moss

Tricky work

In my youth I attended Sir William Turner's Grammar School, Redcar, and my French teacher was Polish. His name was Pietrowski and, as he was always informing us, he was 'Polish by birth, French by education and English by choice.' At the start of our class it was the custom for all boys to be at their desks and stand on the entrance of the master and collectively say 'Good morning' or 'Good afternoon' as the case may be. By accident one day I was performing a trick and the class gathered around as Pietrowski entered, and we scrambled back to our desks. 'Vot ees goints on?' he demanded, and I explained that magic was my hobby and I had been doing a trick. 'Show me!' he said, and when I did the trick, 'do it again!' I did it again and again and again . . . and so it became the practice whenever a French lesson was due to start that we would all gather around and scramble back to our seats, and he would ask to see the trick. This went on for a whole year, and could it be the reason why my magic is so good and my French is so bad?

Paul Daniels

Not nice

Maths and social studies were taught by a friendly but decidedly overweight young woman named Miss Day. One afternoon she asked 'Which elephant has the big ears, the African or the Indian?'

I did the naughtiest thing I have ever done in my life. I raised my hand, without even knowing the answer, and when called on by Miss Day replied 'You're an elephant yourself!' This was a pathetic attempt at humour. I still shudder recalling the silence that fell upon the room and all eyes turning to me sitting at the back.

'Don't you ever be so rude again!' Miss Day ordered. 'Now answer the question.' I guessed . . . wrongly!

After class I was made to apologise personally by my third grade teacher, Miss Charlton. Perhaps as punishment for my naughtiness, I still don't know which elephant has the big ears, but I have never forgotten how cruel I was to Miss Day.

Paul Gambaccini

The advice he gave to Mrs Worthington

A very moving note arrived at my dressing room one day, when I did *Lady be Good*. My headmaster, Marten Walker, had always been very proud of me. Unfortunately, he was too ill to come to the show but he sent a message to say that I was one of his students that made him feel really proud.

This sparked off the memory of when he had organised my careers interview, a very important step for me because it's never easy to get started in show business and I think perhaps it was even harder at that time. Anyway, my mother got me all togged up looking smart and off we went. He was very serious and impressed me greatly, until he asked if I had any definite idea about the kind of profession I might like to be in when I soon left school. 'Well,' she said, 'he's going on the stage.' 'Yes', he replied, 'but what's he going to do for a living?'

Lionel Blair

A stitch in time

Being born in Morecombe I soon developed the sense to think about keeping warm when the weather turned cold on us. So I started knitting a woollen vest at school. It made a lot of sense to me. Practical you see. Well I wanted to make a good job of it and I knew that as a very slow knitter it would take a bit longer.

Anyway, as you know, for a woollen vest the knitting is very small and

precise so it certainly did take me a long time to complete it, and by the time I'd finished, it was getting a bit dirty. But I was very proud of my work because it had turned out very well in the end. So the time came for me to take in the finished vest to show our teacher and the rest of the class, who, by the way, had all finished their knitting projects weeks ago.

Every girl in my class had a knitting bag, which housed all her needles and balls of wool, also whatever piece of knitting she was working on. So I neatly folded the vest and put it in my bag and set off for school. On the way, if the weather was nice, I would always play by the dock on the front and the little dog who lived in the cafe nearby used to come and play too. Well it was a lovely day so we played together for about half an hour and then I had to go on to school. I went to pick up my bag and the dog ran over and stuck his nose inside.

Before I could get to him he had picked up my vest and was making me chase him for it. Suddenly he jumped down onto the beach and started to run. I chased him a long way up the beach and after a while I noticed that there was a long trail of wool following the dog. He looked a bit like that Andrex advert except there wasn't a trace of toilet paper, but wool instead. We seemed to run for miles and miles and by the time I caught him we were both exhausted. He just stopped and sat down and waited for me to run up to him. He was grinning at me with the vest in his mouth. Well actually not the whole vest, just a small piece about as big as a postage stamp. He'd unravelled the whole vest and there was wool wrapped all round his head. I've never really been interested in knitting since.

Thora Hird

Taking the micky

I was always mimicking the teachers, especially a rather forbidding and gaunt maths teacher – a subject at which I was useless. Her name was Miss Hartwell and I was inclined to talk and look out of the window in her class, which must have been aggravating. I was chatting away one day when she turned from the blackboard and said, 'Is that June Whitfield *again?*' and before I could stop myself I said, in exactly the same sepulchral tone, 'Yes – it is.' There was a moment's silence – apart from an intake of breath from me and the rest of the class – and then she said, 'If that was meant to be me, it was very good!' Hearty laughter all round. But I never did it again and tried harder with my maths after that incident.

June Whitfield

A precocious boy

At the age of ten, at Sunningdale School in Berkshire, I was stung into an unacceptable expletive by a careless friend who had knocked over my mud fort. 'You bloody idiot!' I yelled. I was overheard by Matron. In 1953, 'bloody' was a very bad word.

I was hauled in front of the headmaster. He waved a cane idly. 'Is that the sort of language you hear at home?'

'No, Sir. Sorry, Sir. Won't happen again, Sir'.

He let me off with a warning. But he might well have walloped me soundly if he had known what a barefaced liar I was. My father's language was colourful in the extreme and by the age of ten I knew all the really bad words. And, I may say, I knew *what they meant.*

Ian Ogilvy

A friend indeed

I had been delegated to organise my class end of term party piece. I was about ten and the current rage (before the days of T.V.) was 'Dick Barton Special Agent' on the radio. I decided to write a short one-act play – 'highly satirical' (my description not anyone else's) based loosely on this favourite character, I called it 'Dick Bathchair special patient'. Well I was only ten, what did you expect? I persuaded three other boys and one girl into playing supporting roles. I of course was to be the star! We rehearsed when possible and I bullied my conscripts into some sort of shape for the great perform-ance. Come the day, by some strange coincidence, my three fellow boy actors failed to turn up, sending notes to say that they were in bed with a cold (I even had suspicions that they were in the same bed) and the girl –

typically – at the last moment refused to be in the play! So – at 11 a.m., the time of the performance, the audience of children and class teachers assembled in front of the improvised stage and curtains. I popped my head out from behind the screen and announced that the piece they were about to witness was unique – it was a new play, written by me for radio. I disappeared behind the screen for my expected grand ovation. Half the audience appeared to have fallen asleep and the other half looked totally stunned. The next day three healthy looking lads, no sign of a cold between them, arrived at school and asked how the show had gone?

Brian Murphy

Common sense approach

There is only one Latin tag, 'Mens sana in corpore sano – A healthy mind in a healthy body' I am unlikely to forget. My prep-school master, the very late W. C. Barton, was a classical scholar with advanced ideas for his time. We all learned Latin from the day we entered the portals of his establishment, however young. I was four when I went and nearly ten years later I was little wiser but considerably more confused about Ovid and the division of all Gaul. It had, however, been dinned into me in the interval that translating from Latin was 'merely a matter of common sense'.

Came the Common Entrance examinaton and I still maintain that the printing was not all that it might have been. Looking at the first question my eyes focussed gratefully on a word I knew well, Mensa, a table. The full sentence that I was asked to translate appeared in front of my already glazing gaze as: 'Mensa na in corpore sano'. With a dawning sense of satisfaction I realised that 'in corpore' could only mean in the body of, or literally in the middle of the table. Sano must clearly be some sort of verb I had never previously encountered, but what could one do in the middle of a table, but sit? With a feeling of immense gratification I began to realise that it was indeed true that Latin translation was a simple matter, 'merely a matter of common sense', but I was still left with that troublesome little word 'na'. Obviously this had to be some adverb like 'ut', which seemed to creep in everywhere. 'Thereupon I sat in the middle of the table', I wrote triumphantly. It was a victory for common sense.

Michael Brander

Teacher: 'On Wednesday afternoon, after school I shall be taking an extra music class. Is there anyone here who would like to learn to play a recorder?'

'I can already play a recorder,' scoffed one seven year boy. 'Why, I can even play a music centre.'

Having a fling

I was about eight at the time. Volunteers from the body of the hall were begged to step forward at our school Christmas entertainment. Swallowing nervously, but finding the call irresistible, I made my way to the platform and in a voice husky with emotion said I would dance the Highland Fling for them.

In full view of a highly diverted audience I first removed my tammy, then my coat, then a long string of 'amber' beads of Grannie's, which hung to my waist and might have banged back and forth as I danced, and lastly my cardigan.

By this time the audience were convulsed. I was bewildered by their laughter, but quite undeterred. At last, having whetted their appetites with this innocent strip-tease, I plunged into my version of the Highland Fling, only narrowly avoiding leaping over the edge of the stage as I jerked forward a few dangerous paces with each step (I'd been the despair of my dancing teacher because I could never dance on the spot!). Breathless and triumphant I finished to a warm round of applause and loud laughter. I then collected my clothes and my beads and put them carefully on again, one by one, to mounting cheers, before descending to make room for the next performer.

'I did it again at the Kinderspiel,' I said much later when I was talking to my dancing mistress, the famous actress Miss McKenzie. 'Although I was one of the angels, they liked my Highland Fling better.' I gazed at her face, and dared to ask the question which had puzzled me for years, 'I wonder why they laughed. Do you know why they laughed?' But Miss McKenzie seemed to have trouble with a cough just then, and even had to wipe her eyes, and I wondered if she was laughing at me.

If she was, it didn't matter.

Molly Weir

'Dear mum . . .'

When I was twelve I got work in 'Panto' and it was away from home at a theatre in Glasgow. Well as you know the pantomime season takes in the school holidays, but it also runs on past the end of the school break and takes up some of the normal spring term. Of course the education authority in Glasgow was not in favour of school children working in the theatre.

First of all you had to get a special licence from them which took some organising I can tell you. Then if you got the licence and the job went 'on the boards' they had to make sure that you also kept up with your education. We managed to handle that by temporarily attending a local school in the area where the show was on. There was lots of paperwork and the Council had also booked the boarding house we were staying in. I mean it wasn't as if we, as kids, were ever bothered about missing a few weeks of school.

The sad part was that us twenty-four kids from the theatre had to be put somewhere, but the school didn't really want us. They weren't really interested in us, so they just sat us at a few desks and plodded on. All the local kids were getting on with their schooling, but me, I just sat there and wrote. It turned out to be the longest letter I've ever written. Imagine, day after day for several weeks. My parents couldn't believe their eyes when this massive letter arrived.

Dora Bryan

The school pic

At noon we shoot, announced the fierce mogul;
the day is breezy but it's not too dull.
Would-be starlets flutter – screen test at last,
the contract signed, in a production cast!
This biennial Runton Hill blockbuster
throws its so-so dancers in a fluster;
seldom proves a box-office bonanza,
this all-song-and-dance extravaganza.
    Tall pine trees, far-off cliff-top caravans–
exotic backdrop that impresses fans;
on the lawns beyond the new art building,
whose north wall of glass boasts batik gilding,
chairs are set, benches, occasional trestle–
with which make-shift shifters had to wrestle.
    A good half-hour before twelve o'clock
fame-seekers to the film-location flock,
masses of glowing girls with shining hair,
faces glowering at costumes they've to wear,
freakiness foiled by uniform neatness–
scowls at this are all that mar their sweetness.
Here like sheep they are herded into forms–
manhandling indeed, each miss madam storms!
    Every bevy is then arranged by height,
ugly task that threatens to take all night;
either end tall and short are too exposed,
if centrally placed they'd feel more composed;
the middle troupe displays much bitchiness–
that ubiquitous show-biz wickedness;
these of average height attempt to walk tall,
use lowdown tricks to surpass a rival:
fluff up their hair or loose tights stuff in heel–
anything that may an advantage steal!
    Yet prima donna sensibilities
are mollified at length by wily pleas;

55

the director arrives, camera-man, too,
the scene is set without further ado:
on benches hopefuls hop or flop on chairs,
strike a practised stance or give themselves airs;
old-timers as extras join in the stunt,
sit by young talent cross-legged in front.
    Unfocussed the director starts aback–
back and back – as though he weren't coming back!
But at last he stops, adjusts his camera,
while the posed scratch ear, chin, nose, etcetera.
The trigger's squeezed as all their postures freeze,
but the frieze is rent by a furious sneeze!
Blown off schedule by the big rebuff, crew
are non-plussed by the unscripted acchoo.
    Runton Hillywood's epic 'Photograph'
may glamorise some unknown's autograph;
starry-eyed twinkle-toes can't sleep at nights
imagining her name emblazoned in lights;
if unchosen to rise to heights of 'Fame'
she'll stoop to local soap to win acclaim:
Bodham 'Dynasty' or Dereham 'Dallas'
shot at Blickling Hall or Beckham Palace!

Simon Hyslop

'Sidney wouldn't like it'

Every morning Sidney, my pet goose, would be awake bright and early and walk with me along the lane to the bus stop and wait there until the school bus arrived. I felt very safe and happy with my lovely Sidney to look after me. By this time he was quite large and made the perfect minder. He flapped me goodbye when the bus drove off, then tottered off home. At teatime when the school bus eventually got to my stop, there he was waiting for me. He had an inbuilt clock that kept perfect time for him. He was always very pleased to see me and got very excited when I stepped down onto his grass verge. He would often talk all the way home. I'm sure he understood every word I said.

Well, life was bliss for quite a few weeks, then one evening the hockey practice started for the coming season, and I was picked to be in the school team. That morning I took my hockey kit with me on the bus and flapped goodbye to Sidney as usual. But of course the practice meant that I would be going home on a later bus, not the usual time, and of course I clean forgot to tell Sid. Anyway, the practice went well and I was in great form when we got to my stop at the end of our lane. I was a bit surprised when I saw Sidney pacing up and down like an expectant father.

'Oh dear Sidney, look he's waited for me and he's worried; see, he's pacing up and down.' I was really pleased.

Everything changed when I got off the bus. Sidney was furious with me. I had never seen him like this. He really told me off and shoo-ed me on my way like a naughty girl. All the way along the lane he pecked at my heels and legs, and was in a bad mood for the rest of the evening.

From that day on he gave me a terrible time if ever I came home on a later bus than usual.

But I never had the nerve to tell the hockey coach that I wouldn't be able to stay for practice because my goose Sidney would be angry if I got home later than usual.

Liza Goddard

Earning the hard way

I had a really tough time at school, something which I don't regret at all because it turned out eventually to my advantage – and in any case, looking back I enjoyed it all.

A factual experience around the age of seven illustrates the sort of determination that was beginning to develop because of my lack of life's goodies.

I was on the way, walking I may add, to the British Museum with several other boys from Fernhead Road, Paddington on a Saturday morning (after all, it was free of charge in those days) and crossing the Bayswater Road, I was knocked down by a lady riding a bicycle – not only that but I caught my ear in the spokes of the wheel. I cried, tried not to, but still couldn't help it, and the lady, probably much more upset than myself, opened her purse and gave me 6d. What an amazing blow-dry for children's tears money is. I thanked the lady and waved as I skipped off with my chums to enjoy myself with the sweets, lemonade and ice-cream until I was skint again.

For the next two or three months I spent every Saturday morning by myself running across the Bayswater Road trying to get knocked down by a bicycle. I frequently caused chaos, even to the extent of having a policeman chase me away from the 'scene of the tanner' as I often call it when I travel along the Bayswater Road these days.

I was unlucky. I never got knocked down again, but I think I learned almost as much out of school as I did in it.

Norman Wisdom

Putting us in the pictures

At every school there is a boy or girl whom you adore – but your parents dislike, for either snobbish reasons (e.g. they do not talk correctly, or they don't come from the right part of town) or just that they're a bad influence all round – getting you to do all the things you want to do, that you know your parents will disapprove of.

My friend Samples was one of these. He covered both categories. He talked sloppily and he was a villain in my parents' eyes. But to me and my brother he was the one we could get to do all the things our other friends wouldn't dream of doing, and we wickedly blamed him if we got caught.

One incident comes to mind – 'Bunking into the Cinema'. I don't know if it still happens, but it was a childish practice of ours. Samples would squeeze through the local cinema's toilet window and let us in at the exit door. This became such a well-known weekly adventure that not only us kids but old-age pensioners who couldn't (at that time) afford the cinema also waited for Samples to appear. Sadly, his Robin Hood deed was discovered eventually and he was ejected by the powers that be, while the aged and we his good friends remained to enjoy the film. He never seemed to take offence – it was just great fun. And he thought up something bigger and better the next week.

Cleo Laine

Cheeky pupils

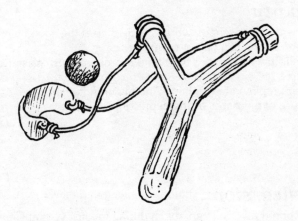

Ageing

It doesn't happen very often but my relations sometimes remember my schooldays, and it's usually something I did wrong. Except, that is, my Gran. She always had the family stories to pull out of her hat. Apparently when I was quite small I was staying with my Gran, and I'd been playing quite happily with some local girls most of the day and the time came to come in and get bathed and ready for bed. You know what kids are like, when bedtime comes around – they will find any number of things to do or talk about, just to prolong the evening before they have to get into the sack. I had run out of ideas when I suddenly said 'Gran, how old are you?' She didn't seem to want to talk to me about her age. I didn't really understand, but I do now of course. Eventually she sort of mumbled, 'Oh, I don't know, can't remember.' I said, 'That's all right Gran, if you can't remember, all you have to do is look in the back of your knickers. It says 4 to 6 in mine.'

Aimi MacDonald

Old party

My housemaster at school (who recently died at the age of ninety-six) said to a new boy on the first day of term:

'Wapshott? Wapshott? That name seems familiar. Wasn't your father in my form?'

'Yes sir', replied the stripling. 'And my grandfather!'

Collapse of old party, as the expression is.

P. G. Wodehouse

Expelled, stop

A boy whom I admired very much during my first year at Charterhouse was the Hon. Desmond O'Brien. He was the only Carthusian in my time who cheerfully disregarded all school rules. He had skeleton keys for the school library, chapel and science laboratories and used to break out of his house at night and carefully disarrange things there. The then headmaster was fond of O'Brien and forgave him much. O'Brien had the key of the headmaster's study too and, going there one night with an electric torch, carried off a memorandum which he showed me – 'Must expel O'Brien.' He had a wireless receiving-station in one of the out-of-bounds copses on the school grounds, and he discovered a ventilator shaft down which he could shoot into the school library from outside and create great disturbance without detection. One day we were threatened with the loss of a Saturday half-holiday because some member of the school had killed a cow with a catapult, and nobody would own up. O'Brien had fired the shot; he was away at the time on special leave for a sister's wedding. A friend wrote to him about the half-holiday. He sent the headmaster a telegram: 'Killed cow sorry coming O'Brien.' At last, having absented himself from every lesson and chapel for three whole days, he was expelled. He was killed early in the war while bombing Bruges.

Robert Graves

A death in the family

When lessons grew too tiresome, or too insoluble, we had our traditional ways of avoiding them.

'Please, miss, I got to stay 'ome tomorrow, to 'elp with the washing – the pigs – me dad's sick.'

'I dunno, miss; you never learned us that.'

'I 'ad me book stole, miss. Carry Burdock pinched it.'

'Please, miss, I got a gurt 'eadache.'

Sometimes these worked, sometimes they didn't. But once, when some tests hung over our heads, a group of us boys evaded them entirely by stinging our hands with horseflies. The task took all day, but the results were spectacular – our hands swelled like elephants' trunks. 'T'was a swarm, please, miss. They set on us. We run, by they stung us awful.' I remember how we groaned, and that we couldn't hold our pens, but I don't remember the pain.

At other times, of course, we forged notes from our mothers, or made ourselves sick with berries, or claimed to be relations of the corpse at funerals (the churchyard lay only next door). It was easy to start wailing when the hearse passed by, 'It's my auntie, miss – it's my cousin Wilf – can I go miss, please miss, can I?' Many a lone coffin was followed to its grave by a straggle of long-faced children, pinched, solemn, raggedly dressed, all strangers to the astonished bereaved.

Laurie Lee

Art for art's sake

The small talent for drawing that I had discovered at quite an early age also caused one of the earliest setbacks in my embryo art career.

Aged about eleven years, I had seized the opportunity of our master's temporary absence from the classroom to demonstrate my ability with chalk and blackboard.

Egged on by my classmates (oh vanity!) I had nearly completed a quite superb, large caricature of our absent mentor.

Occupying centre stage, immersed in my creation, I had only been

conscious and conceitedly aware of my audience reaction. Ego-boosted pride gave extra, confident flourishes to the chalk hand.

Suddenly the audience was quiet. One of those ominous silences crept in. I knew without turning my head – he was back!

The chalk broke under my slowing and now trembling fingers. He handed me another piece and the duster – 'Carry on young Maile; let us see how good you are with algebraic equations.'

Time draws a discreet veil over such events but suffice to say there was just and painful retribution.

Ben Maile

Ewell Boys' School 1938

One morning, going back up the stone stairs to the classroom, I looked behind and saw Mickey Wall making his way alone across the playground. It was a strange sight. He waddled forward, flapping his arms vigorously up and down against his sides like a penguin about to take impossible flight. His concentraton was fierce and exhilarated. His palms pumped against his shorts in a deliberate, slow-motion rhythm. 'Wall, what do you think you're doing, for God's sake?' Mr Blundell's parade-ground bellow was startled. Mickey Wall's r.p.m. increased as he swooped downwards. 'I'm just flapping, sir.' 'What d'you mean, you're flapping?' 'I'm *flapping*, sir. I do it all the time.' Mr Blundell's sneer turned to distaste and then discomfort as if he had seen something very nasty indeed. 'Well, whatever it is, stop doing it. You're just looking bloody silly.' 'Yes, sir,' came the cheerful reply. If Mr Blundell hoped for a note of insolence there was none to detect. I had never witnessed such spontaneous and self-assured behaviour. Seemingly unaware of anything but his own joyful release, he did look as if he was having a throughly enjoyable time all to himself. Others might have suggested that he was merely acting daft but he seemed to wander the school and even the streets determinedly flapping, happy and unmoved. Here there must be an unusual spirit. He was certainly unique in Ewell Boys' School in 1938. The sound of one hand flapping.

John Osborne

Aunt Bunbury

I went to a small boarding school in Norfolk where they did not believe in frivolous outings, and when *Gone with the Wind* came to the local cinema my best friend and I, both aged fourteen, knew that we would never get permission to go. We had pored over the paperback book-of-the-film and were both in love with Rhett Butler, so desperate measures were called for.

One evening we slunk out of the school grounds to the telephone box and, trembling, I rang the headmistress. After the suspicious pips I began in an affected and, I hoped, adult voice, 'Oh, good evening, Miss Roberts. I am Carola's aunt, just passing through, staying in Cromer actually, and I wondered if I could take her out tomorrow evening. I know it's irregular but I would be most grateful . . .'

Jill dug me in the ribs.

'And, oh yes, could she bring a friend? Young people do love to have each other, don't they?'

At this wild and nervous embellishment Jill broke into giggles.

There was a long pause at the other end of the telephone line.

'Where are you staying in Cromer?' asked Miss Roberts in strangely flat tones.

'The Firs, High Street,' I invented, 'no telephone, I am afraid.'

All seemed lost, but Miss Roberts gave a limited permission provided we were back in reasonable time. We went to the film and returned yet more in love with Rhett Butler. We told the story of our brilliant coup to giggles and admiration all round.

Two days later I met Miss Roberts in the passage.

'Ah, Carola,' she said with a distinct twinkle in her eye, 'I hope you had a nice time with your Aunt *Bunbury*.'

Carola Dee

Weatherman

I think I must have been about eight years old. I am sure that my friends and I were really into proving how brave we were and how daring we could be if put to the test. Just think, macho men at eight years old.

Well, I suppose lots of kids get together to walk home from school and that's when the fun starts; all larking about and showing off and looking for adventures to get involved in. Strange isn't it how little boys always seem to have been fond of 'scrumping'. You know what I mean: climbing the fence into somebody's orchard and pinching apples and pears. Eating the apples in front of your mates even if they were sour just to make it all worthwhile.

This particular day, a couple of my pals and I were out of school on our way home, with time to kill and looking for some action. We found ourselves walking down the High Street towards the bus station. Then, there in front of us appeared the challenge for today. Out in front of the local store there was a display of fruit and vegetables, very professionally presented to make your mouth water. Why bother climbing walls or fences, and then having to climb the trees to get at the apples when here they were all laid out? Polished up and ready to be polished off. Easy scrumping if ever we saw it.

We huddled round and made our plans like some American football team setting the play. It was decided, after heavy debate, that a rush attack would be the best method, then we would disperse and re-form later at the local church cemetery to share out the swag. Casually we strolled down the pavement towards the shop, and suddenly the command was given.

We hit quickly and smoothly; no noise. We grabbed, stuffed up our jumpers and ran. It was all over in seconds, as good as the SAS. Heart pounding, I made my way to the rendezvous point. The other two were already there. We met up, checked that we were not being observed, and then discussed the mission.

We all agreed that we were petrified and would never ever do anything like that again. We all blamed each other for suggesting the thing in the first place, but couldn't agree in the end whose idea it was anyway.

Still we had the booty to share out. The others produced an apple each. In my blind panic of nerves at the time I had grabbed a beetroot.

Francis Wilson

Good labour relations

At the age of five I quickly realised that being at kindergarten with the nuns was cutting me off from the real world, where the interesting things happened, and it was a relief to find that there were a couple of hours after

---

Headmaster: 'James, why do you answer me by asking another question?'
James: 'Do I Sir?'

---

school when the two local council workmen I had been studying in my pre-school days could still be watched at their tasks.

One was a benevolent pipesmoker in a peaked cap, who would come slowly past the school standing in the body of his Stevens Steamroller on his way back to the depot. If you waved he would wave back, or at least nod. He always seemed to be very old, perhaps because of his consistent immobility, except when he had to do a rapid twenty turns on his handwheel, to achieve a fractional change in direction. I used to stand as near as possible to his line of travel, just to feel the vibration of the ground through the soles of my sensible sandals.

The other workman you would see doing more vigorous things, like re-laying a paving stone, or thumping bits of tarmac into potholes, snorting while he did it, and never saying anything or paying you any attention. He had a large beer-belly, and always wore the same thing – a dark blue shirt, brown corduroys, and a heavy leather belt that would sometimes creak as he moved. He looked generally grumpy, for no reason I could fathom.

Protectively forbidden a two-wheel bike, 'because of the cars', I used to scout around for any interesting action in my own blue Triang motor car, a vehicle I reckoned superior to the general run of kiddycars with their creaky push-pedals: mine had proper pedals and chain inside, like a bike, which made it speedier and more silent. Over asphalt it ran very quietly. We had a strip of this asphalt that ran the length of the otherwise muddy lane behind the back gardens of the houses in our road, and thus it was that one afternoon I came upon the fat grumpy workman, quietly from behind.

He had a drain grid up, and was clearing old leaves and gunge out of the pipe. A smelly old pile of material showed partial success at least, but more interesting to me was the collection of crowbars and other gear that were ranged on the ground behind him as he worked and snorted, in particular the wooden drainrods with their brass screw-ends. A few feet in front of me were large brown corduroy buttocks, bent over in concentration.

What followed was totally untypical. Normally my inclination is to let opportunities slide away out of my grasp before I manage to recognise them. I may have been caught up in a powerful sense of dramatic inevitability, or some other such likely old tale.

But on this occasion I stepped lightly out of my car, picked up one of the drain rods, and whacked him squarely across the bottom. I cannot speak with any authority about the fat workman's reaction: I dropped the drain rod and before it hit the ground was springing frantically into my car, to pedal off in a fever of fear, away along the asphalt path, round the bend, coasting in panic down a slope, before making the long roundabout trek to get home through the front gate.

Whatever possessed me? Was it perhaps a cry for attention? Such excuses were not yet fashionable: if you tried it in those days you were told not to be a notice-box. In any case, I kept pretty quiet about it, particularly at the kindergarten, in case someone were to come round making inquiries about a boy in a blue car. I wonder if the incident was in the back of my mind when later in life I wrote 'I'm alright Jack'.

Alan Hackney

Sweet or dry?

One of the better Heads of House I had when housemastering at Pinkie House, Loretto in the 70s was a young man who was going through his 'Trotskyite' phase at the time. There was to be no decadent western pop music down his study corridor and he had the strength of character to convert his fellow sixth formers to classical music. He was also a connoisseur of tea and coffee. In a school that was actively keen on games he would, whenever possible, spend summer afternoons ostentatiously drinking china tea and painting in the walled garden. Friends would drift by to admire his work and were rewarded with a small cup of china tea. All this was easily observed from my drawing room window – it was several years later that I discovered that the teapot was dispensing not tea but sherry.

Incidentally, the young man won his place at Cambridge, where he gained a first, and is now the *Scotsman's* parliamentary correspondent.

P. H. Lapping

Macbeth on the move

On a particular occasion he was teaching that part of 'Macbeth' in which it appeared that 'Birnam wood moved towards Dunsinane.' The class was enjoying the master's performance immensely and duly clapped and cheered.

I was in an adjacent classroom separated by a thin wooden partition with an ample peephole. Previously I had swopped several sheets of blotting paper for a huge magnet. During the break period which preceded the literature lesson I had placed a detachable pen nib on one side of the partition with my magnet positioned on the other side of the partition.

During the performance of Macbeth, each time the master took the part, either of the moving bushes or the grimacing Macbeth, I moved my magnet and the pen nib duly moved in sequence to the master's actions. This drew tremendous laughter next door which the master attributed to his acting ability. He responded by overacting even more and the laughter increased accordingly.

I was enjoying the episode to such an extent that I could not conceal my own enjoyment and was in fits of laughter.

By this time my own class was in an uproar and my master who had shared the amusement had sent for the headmaster. He too shared the humour but not immediately. My first realisation was a tap on the shoulder followed by a pointing towards the study and a subsequent receiving of 'three of the best.'

My vivid memory of the entire event includes my returning to my own classroom and demanding the return of my blotting paper.

A. C. Partridge

I say, I say, I say

Once upon a time there were no ball-point pens. You don't have to go back to Charles Dickens for this because even when I was at school in the 1930s we had to use ink. And, during the ink age, the novelty shops used to sell cardboard ink blots which looked very realistic. The boys decided to try this out on a grumpy old teacher like the one in the Giles cartoons, and put a large cardboard ink blot on his table by the blackboard. He fell for it and tried to blot it up with blotting paper – roars of laughter – furious teacher. Next day, there was the ink blot again. You fools! he roared, slapping down his palm and sweeping it off the table. Only this time the ink blot was real.

Dr R. Clutterbuck

From bad to worse

I found a world of cleanliness and kindly masters; motherly matrons; green playing fields; a lake; delicious food and a swimming pool. In short . . . schoolboy heaven.

The only grown-ups who hit me were the headmaster who, under great provocation, occasionally uncorked a dose of the cane; and a dear old gentleman who taught divinity, called Mr. Hodgson, who sometimes brandished a clothes brush known as 'Dixon and Parker' because if, as rarely happened, he hit someone with it, the name of the maker was left imprinted on the bum.

. . . I could not believe that life could be so perfect. . . The whole thing went to my head.

Almost nine, I became something of a clown. This was hastened on when, for some strange reason, my balls dropped three years earlier than they should have done.

I was in the choir at the time, the possessor of a voice of guileless purity. Sometimes I was entrusted with solo passages and it was on such an occasion, and in front of a full house, that disaster struck.

Ascot Sunday – parents staying for the race meeting in smart country houses nearby had filled the chapel to capacity. Alone, I was piping my way through 'There is a green hill far away, without a city wall'. . . . Suddenly, on the word 'wall' a fearful braying sound issued from the angelic face of the soloist. I tried for the note again: this time it sounded like a Rolls-Royce klaxon of the period. The paper-thin discipline of the choir quickly disintegrated . . . repressed laughter became contagious and finally, general.

Immediately after chapel, I was caned by the headmaster – Sammy Day. He had once played cricket for England and still had one of the best late cuts in the business. It hurt a lot and, considering the medical evidence that was from then on permanently with me, was rather unfair.

After the sudden descent of my testicles, I was removed from the choir as a bad risk and became the 'bellows man' and the musical success of each service (we suffered through two a day) depended entirely on my prowess behind the organ. This was a position of great trust, but the newly found clown in me could not resist the opportunities it offered. For a small price – two chocolate whirls, one Cadbury's Milk Flake or a brace of Turkish delights – I could be bribed to let the air out of the bellows on important occasions. The whole school, on the selected day, would be in the know and would sit through an endless sermon hugging itself with delicious anticipation.

It took careful preparation but I could generally arrange matters so that a rude noise could be subtly injected into the proceedings, usually just after an Amen. I could redress the situation rapidly by quick pumping and only the connoisseurs could detect that it was not a mistake . . . the boys were all connoisseurs.

Once I tried it when the Bishop of Ripon was in the middle of a special address. This was my masterpiece and also my downfall but the bribes were mountainous.

It was a highly technical job and involved surreptitiously and noiselessly keeping the bellows half-filled for several minutes after the end of the preceding hymn. I had intended to let this air out in a series of well-spaced small squeaks and trills thus keeping the boys happy during what promised to be a long, trying period, but something went wrong and it all came out at once and on a most unfortunate cue . . . a quotation from Proverbs 7, 'I have perfumed my bed with myrrh, aloes and cinnamon . . .'

It was as if the bellows could not contain themselves any longer – a tremendous fart rent the air. All was confusion.

The school was infiltrated with informers and I was soon dealt with once more by the long-suffering Sammy Day.

I loved Heatherdown and tried hard to uphold the agricultural standards of the landed gentry with whom I was rubbing shoulders.

Every summer on the First Sunday After the Derby (it is not thus described in the Book of Common Prayer but so many boys of noble birth had racehorse owner fathers that at Heatherdown, it far outranked Rogation Sunday, the Sunday after Advent, and the Twenty-first Sunday after Trinity) a prize was given to the boy with the most beautiful garden. Each boy had one about the size of a lavatory mat in a small commercial hotel, but immense ingenuity and forethought was displayed by the owners. Actually, these allotments were status symbols of the worst kind, and boys whose family estates employed an army of gardeners proudly displayed the most exotic flowers and shrubs, delivered for planting hot from the family greenhouses while the more modest smallholders nurtured colourful annuals and arranged them in intricate patterns.

I could only manage a bi-annual crop of mustard and cress.

The year that Humorist won the Derby saw that rare phenomenon, a drought in England, and my crop, carefully timed for the Flower Show, failed, burned to a crisp.

By now the self-appointed jester to the upper classes, I decided to fill the gap, and creeping out of the dormitory after dark, I made my way downstairs and flitting from tree to tree in the moonlight, arrived at a well-known gap in the wall which separated Heatherdown from Heathfield – the girls' school next door.

From preliminary reconnaisance, I knew that this gap opened on to the kitchen garden. I selected a huge vegetable marrow plant, pulled it up by the roots and once safely back on the male side of the wall, hid it behind a piece of corrugated iron.

It took some while and several near heart attacks but I finally made it back to bed. The next morning I retrieved the marrow and in the hubbub caused by the arrival of other boys' parents in Daimlers and Rolls-Royces, managed to plant my prize on my poor piece of desert.

It didn't go down very well. The Countess of Jersey – one of the parents – presented the prizes.

She didn't give one to me and later, I was caned again by a no longer affable Sammy Day: not for making a nonsense of the Flower Show which could have been justified – but for *stealing* which put a totally different connotation on the thing.

After this, I went rapidly downhill from popular school clown to unpopular school nuisance. Striving to maintain my waning reputation, I fell in the lake and nearly drowned, purposely split the seat of my trousers on the school

---

Chemistry teacher: 'What can you tell me about nitrates?'
Pupil: 'Well sir . . . er . . . they're a lot dearer than day-rates.'

P.E. Teacher: 'Jack your feet are filthy.'
Jack: 'Yes Sir.'
P.E. Teacher: 'Have you been in bed with them like that?'
Jack: 'Yes Sir.'
P.E. Teacher: 'I shudder to think what the bedclothes are like.'
Jack: 'They're O.K. I keep my socks on in bed.'

walk through Ascot and was caught trying to get into the Racecourse – a hideous crime. Poor Brian Franks, a Bembridge Friend, near death's door with pneumonia at Wixenford, a school nearby, received from me on the day of his 'crisis', a large chocolate box inside which was a smaller box, then a smaller box and so on down the scale to a match box with a piece of dog's mess in it.

Not a funny joke, especially for the Matron who opened it, but then I didn't know Brian was ill.

Brian overcame his illness and my gift and has remained a life-long friend but the Matron took a dim view, the smoke signals went up between Wixenford and Heatherdown and Sammy Day decided that his school could get along without me.

I was ten and a half when I was expelled.

David Niven

Warming up

I do remember the teacher saying in school: 'I will give a penny to any pupil that can answer this next question.' (A penny was a large amount of money in those days).

He said, 'What is it that keeps England free from freezing up in the winter?' I reaped the reward with my reply: 'The golf stream, Sir.'

Ernie Wise

Stickler for the rules

Hidden away in some subsection of the Winchester traditions was a ruling that all masters, when teaching, must wear gowns. If any master offended on this, then he was liable to have a Latin dictionary thrown at him. Of course we would never do this, nor be so petty minded – but if the master happened to live by these rules, and the same master was making several lives a misery, then, perhaps . . . It all happened so quickly. 'He's coming,' 'He's got no gown,' 'Here, Taylor, take this dictionary,' 'Well go on.' I had no intention of actually throwing it. I was just going to threaten him, but once his beaming self-satisfied face appeared at the door, something went snap in my mind. That dictionary didn't just fly, it rocketed. Any baseball team in the world would have signed me on immediately as their number one pitcher. It caught him plum on the forehead from right across the room. The dictionary seemed to explode into a thousand tiny pieces. I don't think it hurt him physically, but mentally, that was a different story. The complexity of reactions that crossed his face was a marvel. With total silence in the classroom he went from surprise, to anger, to extreme anger and then the excruciatingly painful realization that he'd been caught at his own game. He controlled himself superbly and started to put his gown on, looking down as

70

he did so. At this moment his control went altogether. Why now, I thought? It was then that someone whispered to me, 'It was *his* Latin dictionary you threw.'

Tim Brooke-Taylor

Music to our ears

My years at Abinger Hill were, on the whole, relatively happy. The boys there were very much out of the ordinary, with a high proportion of eccentrics and sophisticates. I remember my lot of new boys included a rather fat eight-year-old whose *sangfroid* was such as to be unforgettable. Our first class was taken by the headmaster, who, in order to put us at our ease, read out an extract from, I think, one of Macaulay's essays. It was totally above my head but agreeable to listen to. After about twenty minutes he stopped, and asked us whether we had any questions. None of us had. We were all, naturally enough, tongue-tied, except for this fat eight-year-old, who was sitting next to me. To my astonishment, up went his podgy little hand. 'Yes, Edward,' said the headmaster, who was progressive even to the point of using Christian names, which in those days was highly unconventional. 'What is your question?' 'Not really a question, Sir,' said my neighbour, 'more an observation. I just wanted to tell you that with your voice you could fill the Albert Hall.' The boy's name was Edward Boyle.

Peregrene Worsthorne

Say please!

At the beginning of the art lesson, I was putting out the paints for the children to use, when a rather demanding five-year-old lad pointed to a pot of paint and said, 'I want that one!' I told the child he could have any paint he wanted provided he said the magic word.

He then pointed to another pot of paint and said, 'I want that one!' I then repeated my instruction regarding using the magic word and said then he could have two or three different pots of paint.

He then looked at me rather strangely and said 'Abracadabra! I want that paint, that paint and that paint!'

Shirley Muggeridge

Making one's mark

The convent school I attended had gone to enormous pains to raise enough money to buy six new chapel pews. The day finally arrived when they were proudly installed in the chapel.

71

Shortly after that I went to chapel and during the habitual daily routine of the, in those days meaningless prayers, absent mindedly I sunk my teeth into the book ledge of the new pew in which I knelt. Having done this in several different places, I eventually noticed that sizeable impressions were being left on the ledge.

The following morning in 'Assembly' the headsister said she had something of extreme seriousness to say.

'Someone – someone, has had the audacity to – to bite a new chapel pew . . . I want whoever it was to come and tell me by the end of the day or I will have the dentist here to take impressions of everyone's teeth, until I find out who did this.'

I spent all morning in fear and terror of what might befall me when I owned up. Eventually at lunchtime, having previously inquired from the English teacher whether it was correct to say 'It was I', or 'It was me', I crept to the headsister's office, fawned up to her and blurted out 'Please, sister, it was I who bit the chapel pew' . . . She was memorably civil towards me despite such a crime.

Lucinda Green

O Wall!

He was ever ready to coin a meaningless phrase or invent a word by the mere addition of a letter. During a long fiery afternoon in Mr Jones's pit of Scripture and whacking, he was challenged about the contents of a toffee tin under his desk. 'What is that you are playing with, Wall?' 'It's my gzoo.'

'What's in that tin?' 'My gzoo, sir.' 'And what's that?' Mickey, looking eagerly helpful, held up the tin and took out the various toy animals, elephants, giraffes, lions, antelopes. 'These, sir. This is my gzoo.' Mr Jones looked upon Mickey's Ark as if it were of the Covenant rather than Noah. The creatures of the pit waited for the fork of Welsh flame to strike and consume the blasphemer. Mr Jones stared, nostrils flared for the whiff of evil. Instead of dragging Mickey to damnation by the ear he flung down his palsied cane and mumbled, 'Well, put it away again. We don't want to see it.' Elijah's chariot wheel had lost a small spoke.

John Osborne

Trestle day

'How nice of you to drop in!' This was how my old geography master (nicknamed 'Bread') would greet every boy who arrived late for his lesson. Countless pupils heard this phrase over the years: whole classes would mime in unison behind his back, pre-empting his utterance as a late arrival would sheepishly enter minutes or seconds late.

It was the school's custom that on the day preceding Sports Day, four boys would be picked for 'Trestles'. 'Trestles' meant that the chosen four would have the entire day free from studies while they took the trestle tables – together with an assortment of chairs, a loud-hailer and bunting – out of the attic and onto the playing fields. This done, the tables would be covered with a large tarpaulin and all would be ready for the following day's events.

To be chosen for this task was an enormous privilege and the lucky four would be the envy of the entire upper fifth. Looking back now I can't for the life of me think what was so attractive about hauling large heavy tables from one end of the school to another together with a perilous climb up extremely unsafe ladders – except, of course, for the binge.

The attic ran the length of three classrooms. Once up into it one had to balance one's way along the rafters taking care not to tread on the delicate plasterwork in between. Risking immediate expulsion, large quantities of food and beer were traditionally smuggled into the iniquitous den. After each table was safely delivered to the field, the four boys would take numerous rests and gorge themselves on the food and beer.

The year I was chosen, rain had made the 'rest periods' even longer. A foolish fifteen-year-old boy drinking beer throughout the day whilst heaving heavy pieces of furniture up and down precarious ladders and balancing on two-inch rafters, is eventually bound to come a cropper.

I did.

Missing the rafters completely, my feet having taken on a will of their own, I dropped my end of the table which I and another half-inebriated boy were carrying. It and myself crashed through the plaster. Piles of rubble fell onto desks and pupils below. I hung suspended by my arms clinging to the rafters, my legs dangling over an amazed geography class. 'Bread' calmly raised his eyes from a map of South Wales and said: 'How nice of you to drop in.'

I wasn't expelled but I was punished severely. 'Trestle Day' was to be no longer. It became one of the many non-academic lessons I was to learn the hard way.

Ian Masters

Boy with a clear head

My parents sent me to Harrow and, during a very wet season, rain came pouring into my study and fell on me while in bed. I wrote home urgently telling of this predicament.

My father, Robin Fox, decided to investigate. So he called on my master at Harrow, who had been his fellow pupil at school and with whom he was on friendly terms.

As luck would have it, it was a day of heavy rain. The three of us proceeded to my study and stood beside my bed, watching the rain-drops dripping down. My father was horrified and demanded redress.

After a pause, the housemaster gazed stonily at father and me saying, 'I think you are both making too much fuss. The water is only falling on his feet, not his head.'

This prompted me to enquire, 'Which is preferable? Cool feet or a cool head?'

Edward Fox

'What are you making, Tommy?' asked the woodwork teacher.
'A portable,' replied the small boy.
'A portable what?'
'I don't yet know, sir. I've only made the handle.'

Pupil: 'Can I have a cigarette?'
Teacher: 'Good heavens? No, certainly not! Do you want to get me into trouble?'
Pupil: 'Well, all right then, Miss. But I'd rather have a cigarette.'

The
three Rs

The classics

We are labouring under the satires of Horace. I say 'labouring', and this shocks you for you like Horace; so do I; but you see one sits at the end of a bench with a large book and a small text, and all the while our reverend precepter, who is an Oxford man and believes in Sanskrit roots, and who moreover is horribly nervous and cries out in agony when anyone drops a pen or creaks a table, sits near and listens to someone droning out a translation far away.

Hilaire Belloc

The in language

There was a lot of Latin in Eton slang. Holidays without work were called *Non Dies*, boys who had not passed their swimming tests were called *non-nants*, anyone who was not a Colleger was called an *Oppidan* or townsman. Punishments had particularly Latin names, *in piam memoriam* the law of Rome. Written penalties were called *poenas*, the longest of them being a *Georgic*, the copying out in good hand-writing of five hundred lines of one of Virgil's bucolic idylls. It was a good way of making poetry into punishment.

Yet, on another occasion, I heard punishment made into poetry. It was my first lesson in classical law, as opposed to justice. A Greek master was trying to interest us on a hot summer's day in the trial of Socrates. Attention yawned, learning dozed.

'You,' the master said, pointing at a boy at random, 'will write me out a Georgic by breakfast.'

'But I have done nothing, sir,' the boy replied.

'Exactly,' the master replied. 'That is why you will write me out the Georgic.'

After that, we listened closely to the trial of Socrates, and we understood something of the relationship between authority and justice. He was a practical man, the Greek master – or *beak,* as we used to call masters – and the rams of Greek galleys.

History Describe the events leading up to the birth of Henry the Eighth.

Junior Science Write all you know on a pea.

Junior History . . . Roman Britain Write two paragraphs on a Roman Soldier you know well.

Junior Geography On the outline map of England & Wales provided shade-in the Highlands of Scotland.

Derek Hart

Slang in memory becomes fond. It loses its sense of discrimination and develops into nostalgia. It seems not so much exclusive as personal. To me, the banned ice-cream in the *sock-shop,* which was out of bounds when we were in training for our games, is almost as strong in its recall as Proust's *madeleine.* For an exclusive language also gives a fierce pride in belonging to a group. If the clique and its lingo is the enemy of the people, it is the friend of the few within it. What other people called *sending to Coventry,* we called *non-speaks.* For we tried to speak only to ourselves, excluding by our curious reference and silence those outside the bounds of our little group even within our little school.

Andrew Sinclair

Why O table?

'You have never done any Latin before, have you?' he said.

'No, Sir.'

'This is a Latin grammar.' He opened it at a well-thumbed page. 'You must learn this,' he said, pointing to a number of words in a frame of lines. 'I will come back in half an hour and see what you know.'

Behold me then on a gloomy evening, with an aching heart, seated in front of the First Declension,

Mensa	a table
Mensa	O table
Mensam	a table
Mensae	of a table
Mensae	to or for a table
Mensa	by, with or from a table

What on earth did it mean? Where was the sense in it? It seemed absolute rigmarole to me . . . However, there is one thing I could always do: I could learn by heart. And I thereupon proceeded, as far as my private sorrows would allow, to memorise this acrostic-looking task which had been set me.

In due course the master returned.

'Have you learnt it?' he asked.

'I think I can say it, Sir,' I replied; and I gabbled it off. He seemed so satisfied with this that I was emboldened to ask a question.

'What does it mean, Sir?'

'It means what it says. Mensa, a table. Mensa is a noun of the First Declension. There are five Declensions. You have learnt the singular of the First Declension.'

'But,' I repeated, 'what does it mean?'

'Mensa means a table,' he answered.

'Then why does mensa also mean O table,' I enquired, 'and what does O table mean?'

'Mensa, O table, is the vocative case,' he replied.

77

'But why O table?' I persisted in genuine curiosity.

'O table – you would use that in addressing a table, in invoking a table.' And then seeing he was not carrying me with him, 'You would use it in speaking to a table.'

'But I never do,' I blurted out in honest amazement.

'If you are impertinent, you will be punished, and punished, let me tell you, very severely,' was his conclusive rejoinder.

Winston Churchill

Stirring stuff

In a big Liddell and Scott Greek lexicon in a public library I found a page of pencilled notes, in a goodish female (I guess) handwriting.

MY GREEK PRACTICE

πᾱθο-κτόνος	– killing passions
παιδο-τρόφος	– rearing boys
παρθενό-σφᾱγος	– streams of slaughtered maidens' blood
περιπλίσσομαι	– to put the legs round or across
πολυόργιος	– celebrated with many orgies
σηπία	– the cuttle fish or squid.

I sometimes try to build a story with these words, but never get far. I wonder what it was all about?

Richard Usborne

A lit-tle learn-ing

I was taught to read with the aid of a splendid little volume called *Reading Without Tears, or a Pleasant Mode of Learning to Read,* by the Author of *'Peep of Day'*, &c. It was published in 1861 and deserves reprinting. Where I was concerned, it did its job swiftly and, as promised, painlessly; but the other day I looked through it again, and wondered. Here are two extracts:

What is the mat-ter with that lit-tle boy?

He has ta-ken poi-son. He saw a cup of poi-son on the shelf. He said 'This seems sweet stuff.' So he drank it.

Why did he take it with-out leave?

Can the doc-tor cure him? Will the poi-son des-troy him? He must die. The poi-son has des-troyed him.

Wil-li-am climb-ed up-stairs to the top of the house, and went to the gun-pow-der clos-et. He fil-led the can-is-ter. Why did he not go down-stairs quickly? It came into his fool-ish mind, 'I will go in-to the nur-se-ry and fright-en my lit-tle bro-thers and sis-ters.'

It was his de-light to fright-en the chil-dren. How un-kind! He found them a-lone with-out a nurse. So he was a-ble to play tricks. He throws a

lit-tle gun-pow-der in-to the fire. And what hap-pens? The flames dart out and catch the pow-der in the can-is-ter. It is blown up with a loud noise. The chil-dren are thrown down, they are in flames. The win-dows are bro-ken. The house is sha-ken.

Mis-ter Mor-ley rush-es up-stairs. What a sight! All his chil-dren ly-ing on the floor burn-ing. The ser-vants help to quench the flames. They go for a cab to take the chil-dren to the hos-pit-al. The doc-tor says, 'The chil-dren are blind, they will soon die.'

John Julius Norwich

St Joan of Arc was the patient saint of France.

There is an injection for TB called GCE.

Wellington House Academy

Dickens describes it as remarkable for white mice. He says that red-polls, linnets, and even canaries were kept by the boys in desks, drawers, hat-boxes and other strange refuges for birds; but that white mice were the favourite stock, and that the boys trained the mice much better than the master trained the boys. He recalled in particular one white mouse who lived in the cover of a Latin dictionary . . . who might have achieved greater things but for having the misfortune to mistake his way . . . when he fell into a deep inkstand and was dyed black and drowned.

John Forster

Alfred Mond rejects his masters

In chapel for the first time, completely unprepared, his trained reasoning violently rejected the story of the Virgin birth and, from there, all religious instruction. Reared in an atmosphere of adult discussion in which he had always been encouraged to join, he argued with his housemaster until, to his disgust, he learned that the man had never read Darwin. He was disillusioned again by the standard of teaching when he found that his own German was far superior to his master's.

Jean Goodman

Teaching by bribery

The first school I went to was the National School, Alcester Road, cos Cal believed in keeping in with the Vicar. 'There's no pickins from Chapel,' she said.

Breaking up

A mournful boy at the end of his first year at school said to the Reception Class Teacher.

'Oh, Mrs Webster, isn't it a pity that you're not clever enough to teach us next year.'

The Geography teacher uses the video

'Now, from the Canadian side, you see the magnificent Niagara Falls, with millions of gallons of water falling over and eroding . . . and if you would stop talking for a moment you would hear the incredible roar.'

Discussing homework

'No Ruth – entrechat does not mean a cat door.'

They was always bribing us. There was the School Attendance Prize. The first Monday morning of the new year we was all stood up for the Vicar as usual – in dead silence, you could hear a collar creaking or the softest fart. He stood in front o' the fire and he bellows: 'The reward which we offer for regular and punctual attendance' as produced good results, and we are goin this year to try an extend its usefulness by making CLEANLINESS a further condition for winnin it. The untidyness an dirtiness of some boys, mentionin' no names, is a disgrace to the community. SOAP is cheap,' he says, 'and the new supply of WATER to Stratford will doubtless soon make this commodity plentiful, so I 'ope for good results from this NEW RULE.'

Angela Hewins

There is a limit

Parent: 'Do you teach the boys to speak French colloquially?'
Teacher: 'Well we teach them to speak it fluently, but not like *them.*'

Jilly Cooper

Shakespeare
A man called Bowdler cut the dirty bits out of Shakespeare. When Shakespeare wrote 'Go to' Bowdler cut the next word out and that is why it reads strange.

Teacher: 'What would you rather have, eight-sixteenths of an orange or half an orange?'
Boy: 'Half an orange, Sir.'
Teacher: 'It would be the same wouldn't it?'
Boy: 'No Sir, you would lose a lot of juice cutting it up into sixteenths.'

He was sent, as usual, to a public school, where a little learning was painfully beaten into him, and from thence to the University, where it was carefully taken out of him.

Thomas Love Peacock

Undergraduates owe their happiness chiefly to the consciousness that they are no longer at school. The nonsense which was knocked out of them at school is all put gently back at Oxford or Cambridge.

Max Beerbohm

Headmaster 'We try to get rid of accents. They're a lazy way of speaking'
Jilly Cooper

Let nothing go to waste

Domestic Science at school meant that in the first year I had to do needlework, and in the second year, cooking. Now cooking I got on very well with, and I've always liked cooking ever since. For twelve months, I used to long for the time when the cookery term would come around. Yes, you guessed it: needlework and me didn't see eye to eye.

It's not funny really; I dreaded the arrival of the Domestic Science period during my first year. But of course there was no escape from lessons unless you were ill or had a really good excuse, and I was always well and couldn't think of a good enough excuse.

The teacher decided we would learn to make clothes by following patterns. Everything we picked up seemed so complicated to me. Then in desperation I decided to go for a sort of Kimono style dressing gown. Its pattern consisted of only five pieces as against all the others which seemed to have hundreds. My Mum said it was a kind of 'Duster coat', so she thought we could get some 'Duster material'. I didn't take much notice and just went along with her suggestion.

I think it took me about a year to make it. Everybody else in the class had finished their clothes in a fortnight. I managed to 'crinkle up' most of the seams and all the facings turned out the wrong way round. Must have been a mistake in the pattern!

The teacher gave me a mark to match my results and I took the coat home to my Mum who convinced me it was a really lovely dressing gown. She hung it up in the wardrobe, and we had a cup of tea. Months went by and I forgot about it. Then it came out. Not all at once, but in parts. A sleeve first; then the other one, and so on. Slowly it dawned on me why my Mum had called it a 'Duster coat' and insisted on just the right material for the job!

Sue Carpenter

Thank you Miss Shaw

My maths mistress at Cheltenham Ladies' College was Miss Shaw, a handsome woman with dark hair and steely blue-grey eyes. She was also a teacher of genius. Arithmetic, algebra, geometry, she would explain it all with crystal clarity, and then survey the class.

'All right?' she would enquire.

'Yes, Miss Shaw,' they would chorus.

She would zero in on one round face, blue eyes bright and hopeful beneath a dark fringe.

'*Rosemary?*' she would demand.

'Er –'

Patiently, Miss Shaw would explain the problem or the principle again. Once more she would survey the class.

'Is that clear?'

'Yes, Miss Shaw,' they would reply, and I would add my voice to theirs.

Unhesitatingly, Miss Shaw would bend her gaze upon me.

'Rosemary,' she would say, 'do you understand?'

'Yes, Miss Shaw,' I would reply, smiling nervously.

She would fix upon me those steely blue-grey eyes.

'*Do* you?'

'No, Miss Shaw.'

Without the slightest sign of the exasperation which she surely must have felt, she would begin again, but this time keeping her eyes on my face. As she spoke, the mists would clear and light would dawn. Arithmetic, algebra, geometry – suddenly I understood what it was all about. Spotting this moment of illumination, Miss Shaw would pause.

'Rosemary?'

Beaming, I would reply, 'Yes, Miss Shaw.'

Then, with a general sigh of relief, we would proceed to the next problem or principle.

Rosemary Ann Sisson

In answer to an 'exchange rate' question in which London hotel prices (pounds) were compared with Paris ones (francs) a boy (with wisdom beyond his years) wrote: 'It's cheaper in pairs'.

The earth goes round the sun in 365 days but in leap years it goes faster.

Your metamorphosis is just below your ankle.

St Paul's Cathedral was designed by Sir Christopher Robin.

Roger Baker

The principles of learning

I didn't absorb much knowledge at Eton. I learned a certain amount of history and I remember enjoying Homer, but the trouble was that the masters tried to make all the lessons as dull as possible. They felt that if you enjoyed your work, you were not suffering enough, and therefore you weren't being disciplined. They believed you were not meant to enjoy learning, but to be subjected to it.

Edward James

You can't expect a boy to be vicious until he's been to a good school.

Saki

1st Form Physics – Questions on Density

Q   You are provided with a weighbridge and a large swimming pool of water. Describe how you would find the density of a friendly elephant.
A   (1) It is not friendly.
    (2) I would feed it, weigh its food, wait till it made a mess on the floor and weigh that.

1st Form Physics – Pressure

Q   Why is it an advantage for camels in the desert to have large flat feet?
A   (1) So the sand does not get between its toes.
    (2) So their necks do not drag in the sand when they are eating.
    (3) They walk a long way and would get tired.
    (4) So that if they like to steal a telly and run away the police can't catch them.

Physics Mock O-Level

Q   Explain the meaning of the words in italics.
A   It means the ones which are different – they slope a bit.

2nd Form Biology

Q   How are worms able to move along the ground?
A   They have bristols on their tummies.

Mock O-Level CDT

Q   Design an item which can be used to tell a milkman your daily order.
A   Beautifully drawn with all relevant measurements was a sign saying 'See note in Bottle'.

Ena Patterson

84

A little learning

It is the custom now to disparage the educational method of the English public school and to maintain that they are not practical and of a kind to fit the growing boy for the problems of after-life. But you do learn one thing at public school, and that is how to act when somebody starts snoring. You jolly well grab a cake of soap and pop it in and stuff it down the blighter's throat.

P. G. Wodehouse

The mountains between France and Spain are known as the Pyramids.

The Manchester Ship Canal is very important because before it was made all the ships were unloaded at Liverpool and sent by train to Manchester.

Mary Queen of Scots was well known and lots of people knew her because she was well known and when I say she was well known I mean well known.

A mummy was not a Mummy and Daddy mummy. It is a name given to dead people raped in bandages. Egyptians used to mummy dead bodies before burying themselves.

Richard III lost his throne at Bosworth, but one of Henry VII's followers picked it up and put it on his head.

The science teacher's gone to heaven,
We won't see him no more,
For what he thought was H_2O
Was H_2SO_4!

Essentials lacking

I was a happy enough schoolboy, although quite early I realised that it was a waste of time and something that had to be done for convention's sake. The majority of the subjects were not remotely interesting to me and most of the others I could have taught myself at home. It seemed mad to spend so much time on Latin . . . Nothing was taught about health; nothing was taught about the law; nothing was taught about money.

Alec McCowen

Lessons learnt at home

They sat, with no possibility of lounging, upon tiny stools, the seats six inches square and the handle backs only four inches high. They learnt their alphabet from letters drawn on circular cards in a round inlay box which exactly fitted them labelled 'A picture Alphabet for a good Child' with a positively terrifying representation of an old hag in a vast bonnet instructing the luckless infant on the lid. Sums were done on a slate with long thin slate pencils kept in a patterned paper box which states it was for 'A diligent Child.'

Geography was more interesting, as all the maps appear to have been made as puzzles. There were three complete ones of England, France, and the World as two halves of the globe. The English one was published in 1783, and the other two were much of the same date. The world was better portrayed than might have been expected, except that Australia (called New Holland) was a very strange shape with Tasmania joined to the main land and a certain vagueness about the coastline. It was, of course, entirely

---

Hamlet is one of the set plays for the examination and we presented scenes from the play for the parents on Open Day. No doubt some of them had seen it before but they laughed all the same.

Homer's writings include *Paradise Lost* and *Homer's Essays* which some people say were not written by Homer but by another man of the same name.

The gas that is given off is very harmful to human beings and the following experiment should therefore only be performed by a teacher.

An inclined plane is a plane that inclines and if the experiment is successful then the result is inevitable.

Q How would you measure the height of a tall building using an aneroid barometer?
A I would lower the barometer from the top on the end of a piece of string and then measure the string.

---

lacking any towns except Botany Bay. Cook's voyages were marked with great care. South America was also swollen out in the wrong places and strangely desert-like in appearance. The Easy Grammar of Geography published in 1815 disposed of the Continents very briefly –

'Africa is the Country of Monsters. Every species of noxious and predatory animal reigning undisturbed in the vast deserts of that continent, and being multiplied by the sultry heat of the climate. Even man in this quarter of the world exists in a state of lowest barbarism.' Asia was also put firmly in its place –

'In Asia our first parents were created, it became the nursery of the world after the deluge. The Christian religion though first promulgated in Asia has been long banished from it.'

Amongst the improving books was a curious set of about two dozen cards with a little print on the top and a verse beneath on the various sins – or at least on those likely to be mentioned in the genteel society of young ladies! The one on retaliation showed a knee-breached and plume-hatted gentleman shooting a dove in an oak tree while a serpent curls round his ankle. The verse below runs:

A Fowler in pursuit of Game
Observed a dove and took his Aim,
In hopes to kill her on the spot,
But instantly before he shot,
The adder round his ancle clung,
And struck him with her venomed tongue.
Thus villains while their wiles they lay
Some harmless Neighbour to portray
Into unthought of dangers run
And justly are themselves undone!

Lilias Rider Haggard

87

The three Rs and religion

In the days when the three Rs were the basis of all education, it was commonly assumed that copying out, in your own hand, some passage written by a superior person would, in itself, benefit the pupil. You would acquire the knowledge or the spiritual insight contained in the passage simply by the process of copying. I say 'spiritual insight' because Religion was a fourth R, along with Reading, Riting and Rithmatic. This copying, particularly of religious passages, was extremely boring, and sometimes led to lively exchanges between the pupil and the master who 'set' the work. It was always called 'setting' the work. On one occasion, I recall, the master said:

'I set you the 27th Chapter of the Acts of the Apostles' and Jones, the pupil, set to and copied away from his Bible industriously. After an hour, the master thought he had done enough, and told him to stop; half an hour later, much to his surprise, he saw that Jones was still beavering away at his copying. Again he told him he could stop now. Later still, he saw that Jones was still at it.

'Boy!' said the master 'Did you not hear me tell you that you need not copy out any more?'

'Indeed I did, sir, I heard you,' replied Jones. 'But I was so interested in Chapter 27 that I could not leave off. It is all about a man called Paul, who went on a voyage and was caught in a terrible storm, and I believed that he was certain to be drowned. Yet as I copied on, I found he was saved; and when I found he was saved, I thought of coming to tell you.'

This is a story that I have heard more than once, indeed it has been attributed to Oscar Wilde, although its humour is of a quite different type from that normally employed by the Irish wit, and I firmly believe it is rightly ascribed to the schoolboy Jones.

Peter King

Violence
on both sides

RIP

In 1730 at Eton a boy called Thomas Dalton had stabbed another, Edward Cochran, to death during a quarrel in their form; the scandal was hushed up, the victim was buried in the college precincts and the killer lived on to enter Trinity College Dublin as a pensioner.

The inscription on Cochran's tomb reads:

> Here lyes the Body of Mr. Edward Cochran
> only SON OF ARCHIBALD COCHRAN Esqr.,
> Of the Island of ANTIGUA IN AMERICA
> Who unfortunately lost his life
> By an accidental stab with a
> Penknife from one of his
> School fellows the 2nd March
> In the 15th year of his Age, and
> In the year of our lord 1730.

But the parish register says 'Edward Cochran murdered by his school fellow, Thomas Dalton with a pen knife'. Dalton was convicted of manslaughter but suffered no penalty.

John Chandos

At Christ's Hospital

The sight of a boy in fetters, upon the day of my putting on the blue clothes, was not exactly fitted to assuage the natural terrors of initiation . . . I was told he had *run away*. This was the punishment for the first offence. As a novice, I was taken soon after to see the dungeons. These were little square Bedlam cells where a boy could just lie at his length upon straw and a blanket – a mattress, I think, was afterwards substituted – with a peep of light let in askance from a prison orifice at top, barely enough to read by. Here the poor boy was locked in by himself all day, without sight of any but the porter who brought him his bread and water – who *might not speak to him* – or of the beadle, who came twice a week to call him out to receive his periodical chastisement and here he was shut by himself *of nights,* out of reach of any sound.

Charles Lamb

Unfair

Punishment was part of the way of life at my Glasgow school, something which we accepted and, as far as I can remember, rarely resented.

I was often late in class, and an incorrigible giggler once inside, so rarely a day passed when I did not get my hand warmed. It was part of the scene, and I didn't mind in the least. Except for one time.

It was when my maths master gave me six cross-hands just before the end of my schooldays. I have always had a blind spot with maths, and to this day I am inclined to count on my fingers, and I was surprised because the maths teacher was a nice man and had always treated me with tolerance despite my woeful showing in his subject, exemplified by my gaining a 5% mark in a trigonometry exam.

When I asked why I was about to be punished he replied, 'Herriot, I have always thought you were just an amiable idiot and have treated you accordingly, but now I see that you have come out top of the class in your English paper, so I can only conclude that you have not been trying for me. Hold out your hands'.

He was wrong. I really was and am completely dumb at maths, and even now I have not the faintest notion what tangents, sines and cosines are all about.

Yes, I never minded all the beltings I had throughout my schooldays, but that time it really rankled.

James Herriot

A clergyman of advanced age

When the new boys arrived, they were entertained at tea by the headmaster, who was at that time a clergyman of advanced age with a permanent grin of considerable intensity on his face. I have no doubt that the Very Rev. Dr. Costley-White was a good man, but he was also a big man, who walked quickly, so that the wind would make his black gown billow behind him, while the tassel on his mortar-board spread over his face like a claw, and he frankly terrified new boys. When, during that initial tea-party, he called out, 'Will no boy select the chocolate eclair?' there was no response, because no boy dared. 'Oh very well,' cried Dr. Costley-White, and ate it himself.

After that benign warm-hearted introduction to my new school, my hopes rose, in spite of being what was known as a 'fag'. I was serving some kippers to the prefects in the medieval dining-hall, which was one of the functions of fagging, when Dr. Costley-White swept into the room, his landing flaps down and his hat at a jaunty angle. His smile was spread from ear to ear as usual.

A pin-up photo had been discovered, he bellowed, a pin-up of a woman in a bathing costume, clutching a beach-ball. He wished the perpetrator of this filth to own up at once. There was, of course, silence.

'Very well,' he declared, as his smile attained even more extraordinary proportions. 'When the culprit is found – and found he will be – I shall beat him!'

And then, very gently, as a summer breeze after his squall, 'I am in the need of exercise.'

As he turned to go, his gathering speed caused his gown to billow once again. I had the feeling he would take off as soon as he was out of sight.

Peter Ustinov

A swinging punishment

At Aldo, I received several beatings for several misdemeanours but the final straw came when I broke a lavatory chain. The school lavatories were without partitions, and set out in a nice friendly line.

Having just seen the latest Tarzan film, I thought I would try to emulate my hero by performing his swinging from vine to vine trick.

Grasping firmly the flushing chain of lav number one and letting out a mighty 'Ah-oo-ah-oo-ah-oo aaah' I swung successfully to the chain of lav number two, then onto chain number three, which unfortunately, in midswing, broke, dropping 'Tarzan' neatly into the bowl, one leg in and the other leg out. There I was forced to remain, 'man trapped', until assistance was called and 'Tarzan' was freed.

This was altogether too much for Mr Hill.

'Monstrous behaviour! An incorrigible young man,' he said. I was beaten again for good measure and, after a phone call to my father – expelled.

Jon Pertwee

Prep school bullies

School, Oh God, how I hated schools, all of them, except the first, the kindergarten, the School of the Holy Family. That was fun. We were looked after by a lot of nuns and I don't remember any bullying or unpleasantness. Maybe that was because it was a mixed school and you just don't bully little girls. Perhaps a pull at a pigtail or two, but that didn't count.

But my first prep school! Awful. I don't know what happens to boys when they get in a bunch. Individually they are quite nice but in a gang – well, they become a gang. And if you are at all individualistic, look out. I wasn't used to boys. I was neat and tidy, so of course I got ink squirted over my new collar, or treacle on the chair just before I sat down, or some other damn foolery. Whenever I attacked one of the bullies I would be set on by about five others, which scared the hell out of me. I was afraid and, not understanding, thought I was a coward. I couldn't go to my father and explain my feelings as I felt too ashamed and also I didn't have that kind of relationship with him. Had I done so, he could have explained that feeling fear isn't necessarily a sign of cowardice. To be brave is simply to conquer fear. I didn't understand this and was constantly trying to prove to myself that I wasn't a coward, so I went looking for trouble. This apparent belligerent attitude affected my whole life. Because of this I took up boxing, much as I loathed it, as I thought this would be another way of proving myself.

Roger Schleringer

My ratio ultimo

Like all other public-school headmasters, Arnold used corporal punishment to maintain discipline. Unlike other headmasters he professed to dislike its use and expressed a desire to avoid it, 'keeping it as much as possible in the background and by kindness and encouragement attracting the good and noble feelings of those with whom he had to deal'. Soon after his arrival at Rugby he wrote, 'There has been no flogging yet and I hope there will be none . . . flogging will only be my *ratio ultimo*.' Yet when a brutal abuse of corporal punishment was discovered – a small, delicate boy, with a record of ill health, having been flogged to dangerous excess – the perpetrator was not one of the old-style, traditional wielders of the rod, but the enlightened Dr Arnold of tender scruples and delicate conscience.

One day in 1832 Arnold, on a routine tour of supervision accompanied by James Prince Lee, stopped at Mr Bird's class to test prepared work and asked the boy, March, to construe a passage from Xenophon's *Anabasis*. The boy said the passage lay outside the section ordered to be prepared. Arnold sent to inquire of Bird, who returned that the note was right and the boy wrong. But March persisted in his contention. The atmosphere became inflamed with Arnold's righteous indignation. In the boy's firmness he saw himself confronted by naked evil. Crying out, 'Liar, liar, liar!', he there and then inflicted eighteen strokes of the rod on the offender in front of the class. After execution March was off school sick for two days. This added malingering to his sins in Arnold's eyes and the headmaster ordered him extra work on his return.

John Chandos

The first room on the right

The school hall was of early date. At one end an old board commemorating the founder, John Hanson. His crest was a pun on his name. A red hand (Han) in a yellow sun (son). It was the school badge. Along the sides of the hall long seats on which successive generations of boys had carved their initials. In the middle a heating stove where we ate our sandwiches at the break. It was a small school. Only about 80 boys and five masters – the Latin master, the French master, the science master, the maths master – and of course the headmaster, R. O. Bishop, the 'old man' as we called him. We were frightened of him. He tormented us. He did not give us enough time to catch the train home. Only seven or eight minutes to go a mile. We ran our little hearts out. But he made us work. He taught us English. He stormed and shouted at us. His house was alongside the school. His room was along a passage. If we did anything wrong, we had to go to his room – 'the first room on the right' – where he inflicted the appropriate punishment.

Lord Denning

One of life's lessons

I happened to be in a form which was noted for its exuberance, and its rough handling of the unwary teacher. One particular afternoon we decided to play a prank – a word not indigenous to a Swansea secondary school, indeed until I read *The Magnet* I thought it was Chinese for a piece of wood. The victim was the maths master, a bibulous gentleman who would come back from a liquid lunch, set us some work to do and promptly fall asleep with his mortar board over his face and his feet on the desk. On this day we waited impatiently for him to go to sleep. When he had done so we blew sneezing powder around the room, dropped two stink bombs and as a pièce de résistance placed a beautifully made imitation of a pile of dog droppings on his open book. Awakened by the sneezing and the smell, he took the mortar board from his face and prepared for battle. However, the sight of the mess on his book unhinged him and he fled the classroom whooping like a Red Indian.

Vengeance was swift, and soon the headmaster faced a flushed, frightened form. 'Come out the boys who did this,' he hissed, glasses glinting. In true Harry Wharton style I stood up and went forward to the front of the class. 'I dropped a stink bomb, Sir,' I said.

'Of course,' said the headmaster enigmatically. 'Anybody else?' I moved aside to make room for the others but nobody volunteered. Twice the head repeated his request, and still no one came forward. 'Am I to believe that there is only one honest boy in the form?' I held my head high, as the rest of the boys shuffled their feet and whistled tunelessly. 'All right,' said the beak. 'You're all on detention until further notice. You, Secombe, come with me.'

I left smugly, expecting a lecture and nothing more. When we got to his study the head turned on me in fury. 'You're not honest, you're damned stupid,' he said. 'Bend over.'

It was then that I realised that the truth does indeed hurt.

Sir Harry Secombe

A pitiful sight

When I was a small boy at the Strand school in south London I was, for one reason or another, constantly getting into trouble and receiving the sort of punishment handed down through the generations, being kept in late and receiving hundreds of lines. But one day, for a misdemeanour that has now totally escaped my memory, I was ordered to be caned. On these occasions part of the ceremony was having to go to the headmaster's study, knock on the door and, on being admitted, request from the headmaster; 'The cane and book, please Sir.' The look on his face was punishment enough and I was petrified.

By the time I had got back to the classroom, wandering miserably down the corridors clutching the infamous cane and book, my legs had turned to jelly and my face was totally ashen. Such a pitiful sight did I present that the master who was about to deliver the punishment said that he'd never seen such a ghastly sight and that it wasn't worth his wasting his energy on me. You can imagine my relief.

David Jacobs

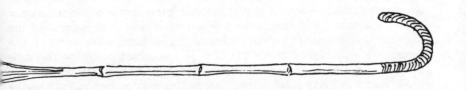

A first flogging

A first experience which begins by being equivocal is described by 'Charley Norton' (or rather, the Rev. C. F. Johnston), the narrator of the autobiographical *Recollections of an Etonian* (1870). The exact date is not stated, but the author was at school in 1859, and the headmaster would have been Goodford. The age of reticence and the 'stiff upper lip' had now penetrated even into Eton, and not only the headmaster, but the condemned also, comported themselves with as much dignity and decorum as the circumstances permitted:

> I loosened my breeches, and biting my lips tight, knelt down on the block. I was resolved that at all events no cry should escape me, and for the sake of my own glory among my schoolfellows, intended to suffer as a hero. But the difficulty of repressing my feelings I found to be in reality by no means so hard as I had anticipated. The first cut, indeed, stung me a little, and I felt at that moment almost as if I was being lashed with a nettle; but after this the sensation seemed deadened and the rest of them felt comparatively harmless. Even before the six were completed, I had made up my mind that there was nothing very terrible in being flogged, nor were my ideas altered by the tingling sensation felt afterwards . . .

The boy then adjourned to the room of one of his friends to discuss at leisure the enthralling subject of flogging.

John Chandos

Strength through misery

There is no evidence that Adolf Hitler pseudonymously attended an English public school. But it is open to surmise that he talked with people who had done so, or otherwise vicariously studied the system. The dictator's Strength Through Joy programme owed much to the Strength Through Misery practised, until the war he promoted, in public schools. Hierarchal rule, tough discipline, compulsory physical activity, love of uniformity, adulation of sporting prowess, dislike of intellectualism, irrational prejudices, intangible rewards linked with real retributions . . . those were a few things shared. The English organisation was the better. There was some flexibility in its application, and the British sense of humour kept breaking in to humanise what would otherwise have been intolerable.

At Charterhouse (late twenties), the initial misery of the 'new bug' varied according to the house to which he belonged: the greater the torments, the higher the house's prestige. No house could then rival Saunderites in discomfort and brutality – and success. It was indubitably number one house, and extremely arrogant about it. The neophyte's position might be today's equivalent to that of an Athenian helot, yet he could take a perverse joy in knowing that he suffered more than those in lesser houses. Also, he was quick to realise that if he could survive a given number of quarters (terms) – for seniority was the supreme arbiter – he would acquire privileges and might reasonably aspire to becoming himself a minor tyrant.

This attitude, of resignation allied to hope, was typified when a burgeoning head of Saunderites' Long room – home of all but monitors or rare scholars – called together the fags, the helots, and declared that he wished to ease their burden of toil, humiliation and punishments. Unanimously, we instantly rejected this outrageous suggestion. Was it his intention to deprive us of the joys of unbridled authority when our turn came? I think the man, appropriately named Freeman, was decidedly disappointed. Serfs will never revolt if they have a sensible chance of achieving government without effort, only needing patience.

Many of the conditions existing in the Strength Through Misery regime would not even be legal today. Yet it worked. Its participants, and the nation, did gain strength – of all types – from it. We did not dream of a Permissive Society: we lived in a real Promissive Society. If we obeyed the rules, we had the sure promise of a future of comparative freedom, even the luxury of exacting obedience from a horde of serfs – a future rendered the sweeter for being earned by simple survival. The Promissive Society worked. Even the rebels appreciated its merits. I know: I was one of those.

John Doxat

Never confess

In the absence of sex, smoking was top of my school's catalogue of crimes. To be suspected of it led, at the least, to a miserably hunted existence; to smell of it ('in fragrante delicto'?) was counted as equivalent to being caught in the act. Punishment was condign, terrible and swift.' Confiscation, twelve of the best minimum and, at the scene of the crime – hard luck if you were at the swimming pool or in bed, wearing thin cotton pyjamas.

The constant vigilance of the masters was augmented by 'purges' at irregular intervals. These were conducted along the lines now familiar to us from films of the war-time S.S. During private 'Study-time' a particular classroom, selected for the suspicious mien of its inmates, would be surrounded and sealed off. The Prefect of Discipline would enter and, like his almost exact contemporary, Dr Mengele, would roll a terrible eye about the scene in search of suitable victims. After a draining pause these would be sent to the headmaster's study for interrogation and retribution; meantime, their desks were searched for further and more particular incriminating evidence.

It was during one of these occasions, incidentally, that I learned three of the more important precepts for life which only a school such as mine could bestow. These are, first, listen very carefully to what your superiors are saying – it might just be important; second, for credit-worthiness and other purposes, try if possible not to have a name which sounds similar to one belonging to a known criminal and, third, never volunteer information or admit to anything unless incontravertible evidence is produced to make you do so.

However, back to the particular purge I have mentioned. I was indulging my *schadenfreude,* comfortable in the knowledge that I had been off the suspect list for at least two terms when, to my horror and surprise, I heard my name read out – number eleven and last on the list. 'Ten to make and the match to win . . . an hour to play and the last man in', thought I. At least I had time to unload the evidence onto a sympathetic neighbour who had escaped the draft. The next half hour went rather like the last act of *The Carmelites* wherein every twenty bars or so a nun disappears off-stage and ten bars later you hear the thump of the guillotine. As my fellow accused went, one-by-one, and terrible swishing noises were heard later from next door, I managed to unburden myself from what I happened to be carrying (one Meerschaum pipe, 1 ounce of Player's Navy Cut, a Ronson lighter, twenty Gold Flake and two boxes of matches) to my accommodating friend.

Thus relieved, I settled myself until the awful moment came. Bravely, with just that hint of truculence I felt proper for an innocent, I set out for the headmaster's study. A brisk cross-examination produced the inevitable result and some few minutes later we were in *media res,* I, bending over an armchair, the headmaster flexing himself for the seventh (or was it the eighth?) stroke when the door burst open to reveal a flustered Prefect of Discipline: 'Headmaster! Stop! Stop!' he cried. 'You have the wrong boy! It should be Barrett, not Garrett!'

'Don't worry,' said the headmaster with some satisfaction and without pausing in his rhythm (should I also have mentioned he used to play for Sussex?) 'he's confessed.'

Garrett Anderson

Ordeal by fire

At Winchester (and Westminster) the cruelties were more formal, carefully thought out, ritualistic as became a collegiate foundation with ancient sacerdotal associations. There was the venerable institution of 'tin gloves'. 'It was conveniently supposed,' says the Rev. William Tuckwell, looking back to the 1840s:

> 'that a junior's hand doomed 'ferre inimicus ignem', to grasp hot handles of coffee pots, broilers, frying pans, would be hardened by a process of searing with a 'hot end' or burning brand of wood and to this ordeal every junior was submitted. I kicked and struggled I remember when I saw Hubert preparing his implement:
>
> > Heat we these irons hot
> > And bind the boy which you shall find with me
> > Fast to the chair.

But I was captured and my hand held fast and I can still recall the grinding thrill of pain as the glowing wood was pressed upon it by the ministering fiend. It was the prologue to the continuous barbarity which was to walk up and down with me . . . a year at least of college.'

John Chandos

Face to face

The most thoughtful joker on record was the boy who, in expectation of a flogging, commissioned an artist to paint a likenes of the headmaster on the target area of his person. Thus when, at the *toilette des condamnés,* the shirt was lifted according to custom, the high executioner was confronted by a portrait of himself, greatly to his and his attendant officers' surprise. It was said at the time that, with the aid of two birches, the headmaster succeeded in obliterating all traces of the work of art.

John Chandos

My husband – 1972

He hadn't had much of a life at school, because he wasn't all beef and muscle, and he liked Beethoven. As far as I can gather, if they weren't stringing him up by the toes and calling him names, they were writing him love letters, and then beating him up because he didn't have the decency to be queer. It's funny how much time is spent beating boys at school. Even when they're old enough to have passed their driving test. I mean, if it happened in a factory or something everyone would talk about the Common Law and primitive behaviour, but because people pay a lot of money for their sons to be beaten up, well, everyone considers it all right, and a privilege and everything. And of course, the ones that survive all this lovely treatment grow into the sort of men most women can't stand.

Charlotte Bingham

The breaking of William Cowper

He was sent to school and, when a tiny and helpless little lad, he was subjected to merciless torture by an overgrown ruffian of fifteen. So broken was he by the constant bullying that when his tormentor approached he never dared raise his eyes to his face; he knew the coming of the brute by the buckles on the shoes that kicked him.

If Cowper in later life was unable to face the world it was very likely because his spirit had been broken at the onset by this gross and detestable villian. Many a character never gains power because the germ of its strength has been blasted at a so-called school.

George Douglas

School hates

As my first schooling was with the Dominican fathers in Lima, Peru, I didn't learn much, but they did teach me to serve mass.

When the First World War ended, I was sent back to England and dumped at a public school with no education at all. At one of my first lessons the master said 'Open your geometry book at page 6.' I was bewildered and turned to the boy next to me and said, 'What is geometry?' It went round the school to my great embarrassment.

We also had to play rugger which I hated. In my section there was a boy with equal hatred of the game – so we formed our own anti-pact which was never to touch the ball; we put mud on our knees to look as though we had been tackled.

'But I saw you touch the ball!'

'What could I do, it was thrown at me, but I got rid of it at once.'

This led to many beatings and I'm not in accord that schooldays are the best days. .

Sir Frederick Ashton

Sport

Frederick Golightly – schoolboy gambler

The time of Ascot Races was the most important period of the year for our young Blood. His room was literally the betting stand where all the juvenile amateurs of the Turf met to forestall their allowance until the next vacation. At this time you might observe Frederick in the centre of the School Yard, attended by his levee, with a list of high-bred cattle in his hand, which he was discussing, to the great edification of his audience . . .

His duns made his life miserable: it was quite impossible for him to walk up town without being accosted with a – 'Sir, you promised . . .' 'Oh, I was coming down to you Mr Golightly.' 'The smallest trifle would be a consideration.' Pressed on all sides he was obliged to throw himself on the affections of his father who consented to pay off his debts on observing a thorough repentance.

The Etonian, *1824*

Sporting instincts

The village primary school at Langham, North Norfolk, was blessed with my scholastic presence as a spotty ten-year-old. The school playground was (and may still be) primly divided into 'boys' and 'girls' by a low dividing wall of Norfolk flint. There weren't a lot of sex battles that I was aware of but the division nevertheless was there – and contrived to bring about my downfall.

My character at that time displayed the usual small boy's savagery – which I now look back on in shame. I would shoot sparrows with my airgun, twist smaller boys' arms, take delight in quartering wasps with a penknife. During the previous holidays I developed a craze for lassooing and practised long and hard on the chickens in our yard.

Then term started.

There was a red-headed girl in the village named Glenda Sexton – a big girl and a fast runner. It was during break that she daringly leapt the flint wall and zoomed intrepidly through the boy's section of the playground.

I was as usual playing in a corner with my lassoo made of that red fibrous string used for binding bales of straw and hay. It was a long lassoo and nothing seemed more natural than for me to twirl it above my head before throwing the coil as hard as I could in the general direction of the intruder.

The effect was shattering. I felt my arm jerked practically out of its socket with a searing pain as the end of the string which was wound round my wrist tightened and bit into it. I was pitched violently onto my face, grazing one of my knees quite badly. However the sympathy I would normally expect for this kind of accident was very much not forthcoming. Instead I noticed a knot of children, soon to be joined by the teacher, gathering round the prostrate Glenda, desperately trying to loosen my patent knot which was imbedded in her neck.

Apparently I was the first person to be expelled from that school in living

memory – but whether the punishment helped to civilize my character, alter my approach to the opposite sex, or save Glenda Sexton from further molestation, I will never know.

J. Greenwood

A gentlemanlike spirit

I claim for our cricket ground and football field a share, and very considerable share too, in the formation of the character of an English gentleman. Our games require patience, good temper, perseverance, good pluck and, above all, implicit obedience. It is no bad training for the battle of life for a boy to be skinned at football, or given out wrongly at cricket, and to be able to take the affliction quietly, with good temper, and in a gentlemanlike spirit.

Hon. Robert Grimston

Quiet time

The only thing I liked about school was skipping around in circles until the music stopped, then lying down on the floor for Quiet Time. I was very good at Quiet Time. Otherwise it was all a bit hopeless.

Clive James

Wit

As a child, I hated sport. Football left me frozen to the ground in winter. Cricket left me bored to the ground in summer so, when asked to write an essay on cricket I silently fumed.

I wrote at the top of my page boldly 'RAIN STOPS PLAY' and handed it in. The result of an early wit was three strokes of the cane, for insolence.

Sport! Painful, as well as boring.

Derek Griffiths

Public school education

A vast system of outdoor relief for the upper classes. In this system of training 'games were the supreme test of moral excellence', and they were the road to preferment and promotion.

J. S. Mill

Sport's Day, 1982

The most embarrassing moment of my school days to date was the 1982 Sport's Day. I was taking part in the 'Egg and Spoon' race and an 80–metre sprint. I was only eight years old then and quite tubby! I was wearing my old gym skirt which was far too small for me and an 'airtex'.

My race was called out after a while, so off I went to collect my egg and spoon. When I bent down to pick up the egg my skirt elastic went snap! Oh no, I thought but hoisted it up quickly and hoped for the best. Then someone pushed a spoon into my hand and I heard the starter shout, 'On your marks'. I felt my skirt slowly slipping down so I quickly hoisted it up and tucked it as best I could into my pants. Then all of a sudden, 'Go!', and a toy gun went pop! Off I went running down the track, my egg wobbling on my spoon. I could feel my skirt slipping down further and further so I hoisted it up again quickly. I ran a little faster now as I could see the finishing line just ahead of me. I was just a few metres away and I knew my skirt was going to fall down any minute now! Oh no just my luck; my egg tumbled off on to the short green grass below! I bent down and holding my skirt I picked it up and balanced it on to my spoon again, I ran quickly and passed the finishing line with everyone laughing! Why? I wondered, until I saw my skirt around my ankles! I just stared at it and because of the huge embarrassment I turned white then red, crimson and purple! Oh how embarrassing though, especially when the teacher came and gave me my certificate for winning, at that very moment.

I was burning hot inside and I wished the ground would just swallow me up. I thought about the sprint and what I would do then? Hopefully though it was not until three o'clock but then, 'Eighty metre sprint eight year old girls'!

I really felt terrible but no way was I quitting, no, I ran straight to the starting line. I think I will stop here as you can probably imagine what happened next!

Catherine Powell

Sporting commandments

That pioneer of English public school education, Dr Arnold . . . was among the first to see that although our Saviour taught us to turn the other cheek He did not mean that we were not to tackle our man low.

Bruce Marshall

Not cricket

The school chaplain was a somewhat flamboyant preacher. He gesticulated almost continuously, his favourite gestures being an outward swing of the arm from the chest, the raising of both arms in what he clearly believed to be the general direction of Heaven, and the admonishing raising of the forefinger of the right hand. A close friend of mine, sitting in a different part of the chapel, became fascinated by the possibility of the reverend gentleman's sermons being interpreted as a cricket match. The three aforementioned gestures were clearly a 4, a 6 and a wicket respectively, and, with the addition of the words one, to, two and too, three and five whenever uttered this would provide a tolerably realistic score-card!

One Sunday three of us, complete with score-book and pencil, followed the sermon with more than usual interest, noting the 'runs' and 'wickets'

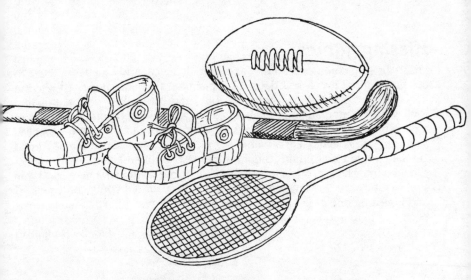

which accompanied the peroration on the theme, 'I will make you fishers of men'. After chapel a comparison of score-books showed only a small margin of disagreement, clearly the odd 1 or 2 having been missed by one or two of us. We decided that the fielding side should bat the following Sunday.

The following morning, however, the chaplain was in a wonderful mood in Divinity. 'I noticed,' he began, 'several boys from this form taking what I can only describe as copious notes during my sermon yesterday. Most rewarding . . . yes, most rewarding.' Turning to our chief scorer with a benign smile, the reverend gentleman asked, 'May I have your considered views on my humble efforts?'

'Certainly sir,' replied the boy, '69 for 5!'

C. H. A. Tattersall

Late starter

As a matter of fact, I was always a little frightened of football. It always seemed a bit rough.

Group Captain Leonard Cheshire VC

Ellerslie Girls School, Manchester, in the 1880s

Beyond a weekly class for calisthenics and drill we had no exercise whatever. That was considered a matter for our home people to attend to after 4.30.

Angela Brazil

Kissing games

I had not long come over to England from Jamaica, and had been going to my new school just a few days. One playtime the kids suggested playing 'kiss-chase'. I didn't know the game, but I did like games, so I said 'O.K.' Well, we all went mad and ran about all over the place. I didn't notice at the time but all the boys were particularly after me because I was a new girl. Anyway, I was having a great time. It took them ages to catch me and I just laughed when one of them caught me at last. Until he kissed me. I was so shocked that I hit him. He was very hurt – in more ways than one – and I was sent to Coventry. No one would talk to me for days. Of course time passed and I became one of the crowd again, and after it was all explained to me, I became pretty good at 'kiss-chase'.

Floella Benjamin

Indoor sports

When I was at junior school the boys were always chasing the girls around, and if they caught you they would often just belt you round the head. As we got older they still would hit you even if they liked you. It was very difficult. I was always in fights and could never be sure if the boys were in love with me or hated me. I still don't know which it was.

Lulu

Rugby Lessons

When I came to Dulwich, some twenty or more years ago, the Rugger Master was John Gwilliam, a former captain of Wales. Gwilliam was built on the lines of Mr Ackford, but strong with it, if you know what I mean. His feet were so big that his rugger boots had to be specially made, and he was a teetotal, chapel, traditional Welshman of immense integrity and charisma.

The Old Alleynians occasionally sought his advice. His comments were gnomic and unencouraging. 'Pull down this Bar,' he advised. 'Build a chapel instead, and a pit-head at the other end of the ground. Then you might have a chance.' They invited him to give them a talk. What about? Oh, Rugby, they supposed. Very well. He gave his packed audience a long account of Rugby School under Thomas Arnold, whom he greatly admired.

I well remember Gwilliam's austere figure on the touch-line. Whenever something ghastly was about to happen on the field of play (and who better than a former captain of Wales should know when something ghastly was about to happen?) he would turn his back on the game with a somewhat withdrawn look on his face. And when irate old gentlemen would rush up to him and say, 'Gwilliam, Gwilliam, did you see what that boy Kendall just did?' Gwilliam would truthfully reply, 'I saw nothing, boy.'

Dulwich Chronicle

Colt colours

I have a nickname, Pinky. There are lots of rumours about how I got it. None of them true. I promise.

It's quite simple, really. At school I got into the 'Colts' and the different rugby teams had different coloured shirts: red and white. My shirt was white, and as usual it got filthy at every match. It was a heck of a job keeping it white. One week I took a friend's shirt home to wash, as well as my own. I don't know how it happened to this day, but somehow they both went into the same wash. Of course my shirt came out pink, and when I wore it to the next match everyone called me 'Pinky' and it stuck.

Well, that's my story and I'm sticking to it.

Peter Powell

A happy little sunbeam

I loved our dancing school and my favourite lesson was P.E. At dancing school we used to arrange all sorts of little concert parties and shows. Of course to us it was like working on the Palladium, but it was very little, really. Still, we put everything into it and our teacher was wonderful. She made us all feel so grown up and professional. In all our shows we would wear great homemade costumes and proper makeup. It was great. Then came the day when I got into 'The Sunbeams'. Real fame at last. I was so excited and so proud. For the first show I did, we took great care over the costume and makeup, and to be really professional I covered my legs in thick brown leg makeup. I looked fantastic (I think!).

The show went very well and we were all terribly excited. I was so excited I certainly didn't feel like going to bed. I couldn't be bothered to have a bath. Then suddenly I got very sleepy and crashed out. Next morning I got up and started to get ready for school. I quickly washed up to my knees with the flannel. No time to wash my legs completely. Then off I went, still very happy.

The first lesson that morning was P.E., so I stripped down to my vest and knickers – and there I stood with two-tone legs!

Marti Caine

Mighty Botham

Best of all, Hibbitt had a credo for batting. 'If you're going to bother to hit a cricket ball, hit it hard. Don't worry about the school windows.' Ian didn't. He opened up his shoulders and once hit a tape-measure drive that was to become a legend at the school. The team was facing a pacy local boy, a fearsome bowler. Milford School's first wicket went down and Botham came to the crease. He soon smashed a ball, right in the meat of the bat, and stood back to watch it. The ball carried the boundary, the school windows, the school itself and finally landed out of sight, in a far distant playground. 'It was an absolutely *enormous* blow,' Hibbitt remembers, with justified pride, 'it would have been a six at either Taunton or Lord's.' Ian was then ten. He was a star. His father exhorted him onwards. 'Dad always told me that whatever I did today I should do better tomorrow,' Ian recalls. 'It was the *next* event that counted.'

Dudley Doust

Dry Bob

A conversation overheard between two eight-year olds:
    'Are you looking forward to swimming this afternoon?'
    'I'm not allowed to swim today'.
    'Why not?'
    'I've got a cold'.
    'Oh, bad luck! How do you know when you've got a cold?'
    'The matron tells you'.

J. E. Maxwell-Hyslop

Umpire out

During a prep school cricket match the young and obviously inexperienced home school's umpire, alarmingly gave six visiting batsmen out LBW one after the other, necessitating a very early tea interval. After tea, he then proceeded to adjudge eight home school men out, also LBW, allowing the visitors to win quite comfortably in a very low scoring match.

When the game was over, the two headmasters conferred. 'Why,' asked the visiting head, 'did he give six of our chaps out, as against eight of yours?' The home school's head answered, 'Well you see, today is normally his day off; he hates cricket but I had to press him to umpire, as there was no one else available. We had words during the tea interval, and I gave him the sack!'

D. C. B. Holmes

Prickly heat

Forty years on, all I can remember of what I was taught at school, which seemed so important at the time, would hardly fill a page. A few scraps of poetry, several mathematical formulae with long-forgotten uses, some dates and famous names from history, a little French and how to sharpen a pencil. What I can remember, with great clarity, are things that were not taught. The smell of chalk dust and the changing rooms, a hatred for rice pudding with raisins, running round the school grounds in pouring rain, or cycling over the Berkshire Downs. These were my real education. One event, that at the time seemed a personal disaster of the first magnitude, taught me something that I have since found to be of great value. It happened when I was in the Lower Fifth and, curiously, it was the biology master, a man much feared by us for his intense dedication to work and his acid wit, who was my mentor.

The Quaker school to which I had been sent, was regarded as 'progressive'. It was believed that our time was best spent, divided evenly between sport, hobbies and our academic studies; the greatest sin was to be caught doing nothing. The nearest approach to approved inactivity was cricket. I enjoyed attending cricket; it was a pleasant relaxation. I have always enjoyed playing games, usually badly, so long as it was not necessary to win. When games become too competitive, they become warlike and most wars, on analysis, are games taken too far.

That year, those who were not good enough for the School Elevens were divided into a number of teams, to compete for a trophy. I was in 'The Seagulls', who quickly went to the top of the league. To my shame, I found that I enjoyed the deference paid to me as a member of this distinguished team by the less well-informed. 'The Seagulls' knew better and made sure that I batted last, never bowled and fielded where I was least likely to be needed.

In my memory, the sun is always shining, the trimly-mown playing fields dotted with white figures playing their different games, interspersed with huge oak trees. It was under one of these trees, whilst fielding at long-stop, that I found a nest of hedgehogs. A mother and her five babies snugly asleep in a hole in the roots. I had just gathered them all onto my shirt front, feeling not unlike the Spartan Boy, when there was a shout from the others. High in the sky, a catch was approaching me, the first ball to come in my direction that afternoon. By the time I had managed to tip the hedgehogs on to the ground, the ball had landed safely for the other side, and they had been able to make the essential runs to win. 'The Starlings' had beaten 'The Seagulls'.

While I caught the escaping hedgehogs again (it never occurred to me to leave them happily where they were), I tried desperately to think of some excuse. Fortunately, the end of the game meant tea and I was so far away from the other players that I could nip onto my bike, with one hand for the hedgehogs, and ride away before the others caught up.

The immediate problem was what to do with the six prickly animals in my shirt. I decided to skip tea (and the 'Seagulls'), and go straight to the form room. I emptied my desk of books and made what I hoped was a cosy substitute for their former home, with grass and leaves. Then I went to get some milk in a saucer from the kitchens. Prep immediately followed tea, but there was just time to show the rest of the form my real catch of the afternoon. None were 'Seagulls'. That evening, prep was taken by the biology master, who was also our Form master that year. His super-efficiency meant that he gave spot desk inspections from time to time, to see how tidy they were and that we were not secretly storing food. One time was that evening. Since my desk was in the far corner from where he started, the form was able to build up a silent tension in the air, like that before a thunderstorm. 'The Seagulls' had spread the story and there was a general feeling that just retribution was about to be witnessed. My mind went blank with fear. For the second time that day, I tried to think of a suitable excuse. Not only was the master a strict disciplinarian, but he was also a fanatic for games; the person least likely to understand how I could have lost the match for my team, just through finding a few hedgehogs. The story was going to be most miserable in the telling.

Eventually, he came to my desk. I opened it to reveal the hedgehogs huddled together and matted in grass, leaves, milk and excrement, far from the happy little group I had expected. The master looked in, looked at me and passed on to the last desk. By not a flicker did his face betray his thoughts. He was, after all, the biology master.

John Prizeman

Girls will be boys

A rather taciturn lady friend of mine remembers, with what seems to be a very justifiable loathing, her schooldays at what I had better call 'a well-known Ladies' College'.

On one occasion, during her sixteenth year, she was playing netball when a particularly vicious opposing forward hacked her most painfully upon the shins. As she was writhing in agony on the ground awaiting some sympathy, a shadow fell across her and she looked up to see the gymn mistress, moustache-a-bristle, scowling down at her: 'Fiona! Stop that! Stand up at once and *be a man*.'

Tony Garrett Anderson

Boxing instruction

My schooldays were confined to the south-east area of London and all three were adjacent to the Old Kent Road, a far cry from Eton, Harrow and Winchester. In chronological order they were Cobourg Road, Scarsdale Road and Walworth Central School. I was always interested in sport and tried everything on offer which included football, cricket, boxing and some limited athletics. The athletics was limited due to the fact that our stadium was the school playground measuring some 170ft × 60ft, not conducive to budding pole-vaulters, high and long jumpers. Our boxing instructor at Walworth Central School was the English teacher who volunteered for the job solely for the purpose of inflicting as much pain as possible on pupils he disliked; it was a form of legalised violence.

Instructive sparring sessions usually finished up as stand-up fights. It was my first encounter with a sadist.

I will always remember one of my first boxing matches at the tender age of ten, it was against a local school and on their home ground. We all got changed into our shorts, singlets and coloured sashes and awaited our turns.

I knew then how the Christians felt waiting to go into the Arena in Rome. Suddenly I was on and was led out to do battle. As soon as I entered the school hall I went into a deep trance, it was the first time I had boxed before a crowd. There must have been all of twenty people present but to me it was like a packed Wembley stadium. The bell sounded and I was pushed forward. I vaguely heard someone say hold up your hands, I just about managed this and stood motionless in the centre of the ring. My opponent could hardly believe his luck, I was a sitting duck and he commenced hammering me. It was not long before the referee came to my rescue; he stopped the bout and awarded the decision to the other lad. I was led away still in a trance back to the changing room. It was fully half an hour before I finally returned to this planet.

Mick McManus

Travel advice

I was 'excused' running in the Senior Cross Country, but required to act as a marker on a bridge spanning the canal just outside Worcester. I paid no attention to the instructions given me, and when the front runners turned up, I waved them over the bridge and across a field – in the wrong direction. The master in charge came roaring up about twenty minutes later, trying to find the competitors, most of whom had gone the wrong way. It is perhaps ironic that I now earn my living as a travel writer, sending my reader in, I hope, the right direction.

John Carter

Making the grade

Picture, if you can, a day at Nantyglo Comprehensive School during the splendid summer of 1976. Carefully dressed in a sober, dark suit I am seated on stage in the assembly hall occupying the place of honour reserved for the principal guest at the annual prize-giving – and I am nearly as apprehensive as one becomes in front of a Wembley cup final crowd.

For besides the 800 pairs of eyes trying to peer at the man behind the tall piles of books and wondering what pearls of wisdom I will utter, there are around me local dignitaries, their shoulders drooping under heavy gold chains of office, serious-faced school governors, and members of staff who two decades earlier could frighten the life out of me with a snap of the fingers. Giants from my schoolboy past.

Often, though, during the ceremony my mind drifts back to a day in 1956 when the then outstanding stand-off half of the day, Cliff Morgan, came up the valley to perform the task I am now undertaking. That event took place at Salem Chapel, for no hall worthy of the name was possessed by Glanyrafon Secondary Modern School, now enveloped by Nantyglo as a result of the introduction of comprehensive schooling. I remember having chosen for my prize a rugby book by someone called Haydn Tanner, whose name meant but little to me, imagining that this would please the great Mr Morgan. But afterwards I could not recall whether he had shown approval or not – all my powers of concentration were bent on making sure that my left hand was used to accept the prize, leaving the other one free to be shaken by our chief guest.

And I think my knees would have folded under me had anyone suggested that one day I should stand in Cliff's place. That afternoon he was a demi-god, a creature from a remote world peopled by heroes like R. H. Williams, Jeff Butterfield and Tom Reid, who had just drawn a Test series against the mighty South Africans.

He, in other words, was supreme in his chosen sport, while in 1956 I was just getting to grips with the business of playing at stand-off half.

David Watkins

A Friendly Game

I cannot help thinking that sport is taken too seriously at most public schools.

Asthmatic, blind in one eye and extremely spindly, I was the only boy at my extremely athletic school to be excused all games. This led to problems too numerous to mention here and which took years to overcome. A brief breakthrough occurred, however, marked by my being asked as a member of the lower 6th form to be the official scorer for the college cricket team. Perhaps it went to my head.

Just before I left a year later a "Joke Game" was arranged between the 1st XI and an ad hoc group called "The cripples", the latter team of which, in view of my new-found popularity, I was elected Captain. Despite the friendliness of the game my team was regarded with some good-natured contempt. However, I knew the rules rather better than my heartier and, on this occasion, more careless opponents.

Having put myself in to bowl first (after all, I *was* the captain) I hurled myself towards the opposite wicket. As it was the first ball I had ever bowled in my life I let go of it somewhat early and it disappeared up into the sky. Stepping back in an attempt to follow its course the batsman I had been aiming at trod on his own wicket which seemed to me just as good a way of dismissing a batsman as any other. My second ball was so far from its target that it caught everyone by surprise and it was not until the middle of, I think, their seventh run that the fielders found it and to one of the batsman's even greater surprise, ran him out.

Meantime I had noticed that each time I had taken my run up for delivery the man at my end started running at the same time as I did. Seeing a hat-trick within my grasp I trotted to the wicket but kept hold of the ball and with a triumphant cry of "Howzat" stumped him.

I had my hat-trick but became a pariah once again. Even 25 years later my last victim cut me dead at a school re-union.

Garrett Anderson

'Food, glorious food'

A Harrovian breakfast

It was a Harrovian practice for mothers of little boys newly dispatched to the school to write to older boys, the sons of friends and known to the family, committing to their protection the newly arrived fledglings. It was quite impractical for a senior boy, moving in an entirely different circle, to keep a close eye on several juniors living in different houses; but duty required from a 'protector', apart from the occasional nod in the street, once a quarter, a *Breakfast*.

A letter of invitation was drafted:

> Dear ———
>
> Will you breakfast with me tomorrow if you are not otherwise engaged? I have not been able to see so much of you yet as I could have wished. I hope you will always let me know if I can help you in any way. Please remember me to your mother when you write next.
>
> Yours very sincerely

Several such missives having been dispatched, the host goes off to order plenty to eat, 'for those small fellows do eat a lot'. Next day, after first school, he returns to his study to find it crowded with as large a table as it will hold and 'three or four small boys sitting on the edge of chairs, looking very shy'. Before he arrived they had occupied themselves in examining his books, pictures and ornaments, and peeping into the dishes on the table. The guests having sat down, after needing to be asked at least three times before they did so, the ordeal begins.

John Chandos

Sixth form tuck, 1829

Periodically the sixth form in college at Eton regaled themselves with a feast, paid for with taxes collected for cricket overheads, when fags had the additional duty of getting their masters undressed and to bed. To accompany the fine fare sent over from the Christopher Inn there was wine in abundance, claret, champagne, madeira and heady black-strap port. At the end of the meal the exalted diners, attended by their unfed fags, repaired to tables drawn up in front of the fire in Long Chamber where, according to custom, they caroused on shilling bowls of Bishop – hot port, spiced and with a roasted lemon floating in the middle. Bishop is one of the most potent mulled vinous drinks ever devised. After a few songs and choruses the boys, large and small, were babbling nonsense, with the juniors, half tipsy themselves, struggling to get the celebrants undressed and into bed.

Wayne (aged six) 'What does vanilla taste like?'
Harry (aged seven) 'Everybody knows that vanilla is the opposite of chocolate.'

Facilities for Oppidans were even freer. A typical party al fresco on 4 June is recalled. 'Meanwhile Jackson had been looking after himself in the same way as I had been, and both of us in the excitement of the evening had been drinking claret, champagne and sherry with the most egregious want of discrimination.'

John Chandos

The 1820s' distressful pudding

Meals could be an ordeal. Distressful pudding was habitually served as a first course to smother hunger before the service of meat. One small boy called Codrington so abhorred the particular vile mess which was served on Tuesday before the roast mutton that he once allowed a grimace of disgust to be seen briefly, but not briefly enough, for thunders of accusation and justification followed.

'*Codrington, que faites vous là? Si le Prince Regent venait diner ici*' – 'An event,' observed Sir Francis in retrospect, 'more unlikely than Bishop Butler's typical improbability that the sun should fail to rise at his appointed hour' – '*Je ne le donnerai pas le meilleur pouding que cela. Mettez vous à genou, M. Codrington, et mangez cela tout de suite.*'

Monsieur Codrington was, as the Reverend William Barrow would have put it, 'without option', and had to obey, while his enemy watched every move in the process of deglutition 'as the spoon tired in its stride like a beaten racehorse' with 'a look of cruel glee'.

As soon as the last morsel had disappeared and Codrington's sigh of relief, silently delivered, was nevertheless registered, a bellow was heard. '*Donnez encore du pouding à Monsieur Codrington.*' The persecution served two purposes: it gratified the persecutor and it disabled Monsieur Codrington from attacking the mutton which was to follow.

John Chandos

Roley-poley by the yard

The Pudding is brought in. Roley-poley again! Now we've had rolely-poley every day for the last three weeks in various forms, sometimes baked, sometimes boiled, sometimes fried, sometimes hardly cooked at all, but always roley-poley. I think the cook must have bought it raw, wholesale by the yard, and when she is pressed for time she cuts off a foot and a half and serves it up in some way or another. She probably keeps it round a roller, like string in the grocers' shops, and reels it off as she wants it.

An Eton boy, 1877

Breakfast at Eton in Dr Keate's day

I was coming one morning from the Christopher buoyantly bearing a plate of sausages (seven for sixpence) swimming in grease and covered with another plate to keep them hot. Meat for breakfast in Keate's eyes was one of the deadly sins, and when, sailing along in full canonicals, he recognized me, he proceeded to appropriate the spoil. Summoning a labourer who was passing, he was about to give it to him when I said, 'If you please, sir, the plate belongs to the Christopher.' Keate was equal to the occasion. 'Poor man,' he said, 'hold your hat,' which the poor man did, and the ownership of my sausages, grease and all, was thus transferred. The plates were delivered back to me. 'You will stay at eleven' for the first time greeted my ears, and the just reward of my iniquities was meted out in due form a few hours later.

W. Rogers

Council school in 1939–45

Every morning, one of the boys was sent over to the baker's to buy hot buns. These cost a halfpenny each and we were all allowed to eat them during our milk break. I think you paid another halfpenny for the milk, unless your old man was out of work, sick, dead, or had left home for some reason. There were school dinners, but I preferred to go round to Gran's or buy some chips or a couple of raw carrots.

Ron Barnes

Evelyn Baring's Winchester routine 1914–18

6.25	Get up, cold tap
6.45	Biscuits and tea
7–7.45	Work
7.45–8	Prayers
8.00	Breakfast – porridge (two helpings) meat (two helpings) as much bread and butter + marmalade jam, as much sugar
9.15–12.15	Work
1.00	Lunch – always very good
1.30–4.15	Exercise
4.15–6.15	Tea, bread and butter
7–8.45	Prep
9.00	Prayers
9.45	Lights out

Charles Douglas

Food at Charterhouse c.1928

Lionel Bart's 'Food, Glorious Food' would have been a song we could have enthusiastically chorused at Saunderites, Charterhosue, circa 1928. A system persisted that would have delighted the governors of the orphanage in which Oliver Twist was incarcerated. Housemasters were given so much per year to run their houses, their incumbency of which had been limited to (I believe) fifteen years. Broadly, what they had as a surplus of income over expenditure was theirs to keep. They had, therefore, every incentive to pare outgoings to the bone in order to accumulate funds.

There were exceptions of course. It was not then unknown for men of independent means to indulge in a vocation for teaching. If one of these well-heeled masters was given a house to control, it was not for him a welcome source of enrichment but a chance to enlarge his pedagogic theories by providing for the physical as well as the mental wellbeing of those in his charge. Saunderites was not one of those rare houses where, by our standards, sybaritic gastronomy prevailed. Our housemaster, N. I.

Chignell (Nic), was manifestly planning a very happy retirement. Under the aegis of Mrs Chignell, a sensationally unattractive ex-Hag (matron), our nutritional requirements – catering is too grand a term – were totally subject to the enhancement of the Chignell current account. Bulk food had probably never been cheaper in Britain: we got the cheapest, and the minimum necessary to sustain life. Baked beans and sausages dominated our frugal suppers; tough meat, soggy vegetables and stodgy puddings ruled at lunch, reluctantly attended at top table by Nic, who was served first. Doughy white bread of dubious freshness was in tolerable supply and butter (then very inexpensive) was available in fair quantity. We provided our own jams and sundry other supplements. Fried eggs, at tuppence a go, could be bought from Cliff, the fat and avaricious toady of a house butler. They were at least fresh. Those provided by Mrs Nic, by repute originating in China, were not. When an embryo chick was discovered in one of these offerings, there was a rare insurrection and it was solemnly carried in procession to Nic, breakfasting luxuriously in his own handsome quarters. Craven as ever, Nic promised reform which did not, of course, eventuate.

Yet we members of Saunderites found a strange solace in our hardship: we were the tough guys, requiring no pampering such as might pertain of some houses. Why, we did not wear overcoats and never ran anywhere – even in the rain – unless on a 'fag call' (doing something for a monitor). What did we care about food! Mostly we started each quarter (term) with a well-stocked tuck-box. I received occasional Dundee cakes from Fuller's. Though often broke, I had fairly generous pocket money to spend at Crown, the school shop. For weeks at a time I lived largely on Cadbury's Nut Milk chocolate: a damned good energising diet for an active youth.

John Doxat

Our daily bread – the 1950s

Kedgeree – I have only to hear the word and I am instantly transported back to breakfast in the dining room of my first boarding school. I suppose I was about ten or eleven at the time. Even though rationing had ended six years or so earlier, the staff still thought that we should be made to realise how

---

A Valentine card sent by one 10-year-old boy to a ten-year-old girl made clear the depth of feeling of which he was capable, admirably:

'I love your eyes,
I love your lips,
But I'd swap you for some fish 'n chips'.

The **Australian**

---

very lucky we were to have any food at all, and must therefore be forced to eat every last scrap.

Complete despair, not to say nausea, engulfed me as I asked the mistress for a small helping. About three heaped tablespoons were put on my plate and it was passed down the table and put in front of me. I sat and stared at it in total disbelief for about five minutes, before picking my way round it and demolishing the hard-boiled egg. I then tried spreading the remainder round my plate and squashing it hard with a fork in the hope that it would look as if I had consumed most of it, and would be able to quickly put my neighbour's plate on top of it, when it came to clearing away.

To no avail, the beady eyes at the head of the table had sussed out just exactly what I had been doing, and so whilst everyone else's plate was cleared away and they began their toast and marmalade, so my plate of kedgeree sat in front of me. Tears started to well up, run down my cheeks and fall into the kedgeree, making it even saltier than it already was, but I managed another mouthful, washed down with plenty of tea. However, this still was not enough for old beady eyes, who told me that she was prepared to sit with me all day (did she have no teaching commitments all day, I ask myself) until I had eaten it all. The remainder of the school left the room to attend prayers.

Silence ensued, and whilst the rest of the school asked the Almighty to forgive them for their tresspasses, I asked Him very fervently if he could please remove my plate of kedgeree. I don't know whether He heard me, or if beady eyes was also chatting to Him and He pointed out to her that if she continued with this folly, not only were we indeed likely to be there all day, but if she did ever succeed in getting it down me, there was a distinct possibility that it might come back up again all over the dining room table, which by now had been laid for lunch. For, as prayers ended, she heaved a sigh and said that if I were able to manage one more mouthful and then would take my plate into Cook and apologise for not having eaten her delicious kedgeree, that would be alright.

I have always been a great believer in compromises, especially if I feel that I have marginally got the better deal. I quickly dug my fork into the dreaded fish and rice, opened my mouth, shut my eyes, fumbled for a glass of water and washed it down. Taking my plate and looking suitably ashamed, I then took it into Cook, who did not seem to find it so unreasonable that someone just didn't like fish and rice, and I scuttled in for the start of the history lesson.

Jennie Reekie

Canteen Supervisor, writing the menu: 'How do you spell Blancmange?'
Assistant: 'B-L-O-M-M, no B-L-U-M no that's not right either – better give them rice.'

Midnight in the dorm

Although my folks didn't have much money, somehow they managed to scrape their earnings together to send me to a great school, as a boarder. At that time the school was a very old building next to the Minster yard. Southwell Minster is one of the oldest in England, and the 'Minster School' was set up to supply and educate the choristers.

In those days we were always starving. Ridiculous really, because the house meals were enormous and good. But then, you know, young lads seem always to be starving. In our bedroom there were five of us, Blunt, Lowdham, Johnson, Heather and me. On one wall was a large Victorian iron fireplace with a sort of flap in the chimney which was closed to stop a draft coming into the room when the fire wasn't lit. We found it possible to wrap up cream cakes, buns, fruit, chocolate, tins of beans etc., and hide them behind the flap, so that when everyone on our landing was in bed asleep, we could get our grub down from the chimney and have a 'dorm feast'.

It was 'Hank' Johnson's birthday and we decided a party was called for so up the chimney went the smuggled food and pop. About an hour after lights

122

out we began to prepare the food. It was a very stormy night and the rain was coming down in buckets. We were all warm and hungry next to the large radiator. We set everything up on Bobby Lowdham's bed near the window so that we could see by the light outside in the front drive. No torches in case we were spotted. Cream buns, open bean cans, buttered rolls, everything was ready when we heard our housemaster Steve Pulford's voice down the corridor; we grabbed everything and stuffed it up the chimney and dived into bed with anything we had over. Just in time before the door opened and Steve said, 'Keep the windows closed tonight, boys, its raining hard outside and the wind will blow the rain in and soak Lowdham's bed.' 'Yes, Sir'. We all faked tiredness. Seconds after the door closed we were out of bed. The food was retrieved from the chimney and as we tried to reset the bed we realised there was soot everywhere. As the door had opened, the flap in the chimney was still open and soot flew down and all over the cream buns, into the beans and all over the floor. We were all black, the room was filthy and the food wasn't looking too good either.

It took us all night streaking about trying to clean up. Chimneys were abandoned as a future food hiding place.

Alvin Stardust

Bottle party

In our school each of the classsrooms had to double, as geography room or science lab, or library, or some other subject. My classroom was the geography room. I remember when we were in the upper school and it was near to the end of the term, we all decided to have a slap-up party. Money was short to buy the goodies, but we had a problem thinking of somewhere to hide all the booze. It would have been fatal if any of the teachers were to find it. We racked our brains to think of a place that would be safe. Then I had a brainwave. At the back of the classroom there was a large sand-pit where the geography teacher would scoop out hills and dales to help explain map reading and how parts of the world differed, in a practical way. The geography room was not much in use at that time because we were so close to the end of the school year. My idea was to bury the drink bottles deep in the sand until the night of the party.

So we sneaked into the classroom late at night and hid everything. The next day, for some reason or other, the geography teacher decided to give the juniors an idea of how they would be using the sand-pit next year. She took her little trowel and began to build up a mountain from the sand. Suddenly, 'clink, clink', her little tool made contact with a bottle of Gilbey's Gin, then a bottle of red wine and so on until she had uncovered the whole cache of drinks. The first form must have been amazed.

Next morning we left assembly and went into our classroom as usual. We froze in our tracks as we saw the line of bottles on the teacher's desk at the front of the class. The game was up, so we just quietly filed to our desks and sat down. The teacher smiled after a while and asked us why we hadn't told her we were having a party. She said we could have put the drink in the class store cupboard and locked it. We were all amazed, but thrilled that the teacher was so understanding. Then she changed her expression and looked very serious.

'Now then,' she said, 'I will only let you have the drink back on one condition. That you let me come to the party.' As you might guess she became the most popular teacher after that.

Sarah Green

Best foot forward

A junior school outing had been planned to a local beauty spot, finishing up with a picnic supplied by mums and friends. We set off in fine style but, true to form, the good old English climate let us down and we arrived in a typical summer drizzle. Wellies and Anoraks were the order of the day but one small child was having difficulty with his wellies. Getting out of the coach I noticed he had put his left foot into his right boot and, of course, his right foot into the left boot. 'Mark', I said, 'you've put your wellies on the wrong feet.'

'But', he said in a rather puzzled voice 'these are the only feet I've got.'

Libby Hess

Military
training

Arms and the man

On Field Days they used to take it so very seriously. 'Now men, if you're shot, then you must remove your berets. Taylor, put your beret back on at once. What do you mean, you're committing suicide?' One particular Field Day I remember with affection was held 'against' Charterhouse. In the morning they had the tank and in the afternoon we had it – three hundred boys moving with this armoured contraption, driving three hundred others before them. Then after lunch the whole procession was reversed. I had the plum job of being in charge of my platoon's 'mortar'. This was a wooden box out of which I was to fire a rocket – a tiny November-5th-type rocket. I still get a feeling of toe-clenching joy when I remember the moment I was ordered to fire at the tank. 'Mortar.' 'Sir.' 'Fire.' The tank was a hundred yards away, my rocket rose thirty feet in the air and landed right in the middle of my platoon about twenty yards in front of me. To a man, with perfect precision, they all removed their berets and sat down to eat their apples and 'Penguins'.

The same 'officer' who had objected to my 'suicide' was also cursed with having to teach science to me and others from the 'Arts' stream. Once a week, for an hour, he would have to get over this colossal subject to a form of very uninterested pupils. This was pure prejudice on our part and I now very much regret it. In those days the science side of the school was fairly small, and treated rather as the RAF had been in its early days – not quite O.K. We knew we were wasting our time and he knew we were wasting our time. In one last effort to gain our interest we were asked to write poems on any scientific subject we cared to choose. He was right in one way – I spent a great deal of trouble over this and my prize entry ran like this:

'Did Newton ever go to Bengal?
No he went to a fancy dress ball.
He though he would risk it
And go as a biscuit,
But a dog ate him up in the observatory.'

All I got, in red ink, was, 'Doesn't rhyme. 0/5.'

Tim Brooke-Taylor

Any volunteers?

A friend of mine, a thoughtful boy called Christopher Benwell, and I, read *Cry Havoc* by Beverley Nichols, a popular pacifist tract on the evils of war. His message was that, if we all refused to fight, there could be no new war. We became instant pacifists and asked to see Mr Belk.

'We understand the OTC is voluntary. We would like permission to leave it,' one of us said.

'Yes,' said Belk. 'The OTC is about as voluntary as being at school.'

There was a way of getting out of the OTC. If you passed a War Office examination called certificate A, you could opt to join the Boy Scouts. A group of us decided to act. We were among the most slovenly ever to wear uniform, but thought we could do well in the written examination if we could smuggle cribs in. The examination was held in Big School. Long lines of desks went from front to back; half the OTC were there, keen soldiers to a boy aspiring for higher military honours. Before we began, the school porter came in with school notices to be read out by the War Office invigilator, a frail and ancient retired colonel. He was so deaf he could not hear what the porter said to him. An excellent start. The next plus was that the manner in which he read the notices, when he eventually understood what the porter wanted, indicated he was very short-sighted. He held the notices right up to his nose with his spectacles off. Confirmation came when we started to write and he walked up and down the platform, peering hopelesly at the rows of boys below.

We flourished the cribs openly. We passed the answers up and down. There were ancient cannonballs on pedestals at the side of Big School. We took them off and rolled them along the wooden floor. Even the good and serious boys joined in the cribbing when they saw how safe it was. They were not going to let us get higher marks than they did: they were genuinely keen on the OTC, the asses. The invigilator was unaware that he was presiding over a near-riot. It was the most enjoyable examination of my life.

After a few weeks the Headmaster said, 'I have a gratifying announcement to make which should make us proud to be Eastbournians. The War Office have written to congratulate Eastbourne on the highest number of passes in Certificate A achieved by any school in the country. Not one failure. We also got the highest ever average percentage marks. Some—' – he must have been looking towards my place, there was a tiny hesitation – 'some of the results are surprising. Congratulations to everyone concerned.'

Woodrow Wyatt

Dumb insolence

Once our whole platoon fell in, each with one boot scrupulously polished and the other muddy. Always we drilled with ostentatious incompetence, dropping rifles, turning right instead of left, making the movement of forming fours odd and even numbers together, and so forth. On field days we either hid from action or advanced immediately at the 'enemy' so that we were 'killed' at the first moment of battle.

When, route-marching, we were exhorted to sing, we ignored the ballads sanctified by the infantry of the World War and loped along out of step droning the American ditty:

'I didn't raise my boy to be a soldier.
I brought him up to be my pride and joy.
Who dares to put a rifle on his shoulder
To shoot another mother's darling boy?'

We were not unique. At other public schools at this time there were contemporaries behaving in much the same way. At Eton there was a platoon which paraded in horn-rimmed spectacles and numbered off: '. . . ten, Knave, Queen, King.'

Evelyn Waugh

On parade

I never disliked O.T.C. parades: as for field days, they were among the happiest of my school life. But it was during the period of the O.T.C. summer camp that Dock and his friends really came into their own. I can see them now – loosening the guy-ropes of the big canteen tent, scaring the horses of nervous masters unaccustomed to riding, creeping up behind a smartly turned-out sentry from another school and suddenly planting a large melon on the point of his bayonet. They were caught, of course, and reprimanded, but nothing more. The authorities were embarrassed: they didn't want to spoil the jolly holiday atmosphere with punishments. The Guards officer who interviewed them, a very nice man, talked unhappily about the team spirit and looked far more distressed than his prisoners, whose faces were as expressionless as their ill-polished buttons. 'Private Dock,' ran the official report, 'failed, for the third time, to obey orders.' That was it – Dock just failed. There was nothing to be done with him and his kind – unless you were prepared to shoot them. The school contingent left camp with a bad name.

Christopher Isherwood

Bugles, bottles and bumbles

My first school was Public School No. 64 which was one of the first in the US to boast a kindergarten and it was here I matriculated at age five in

---

No kidding

A friend recently boosted his income by marking the general knowledge exam at a nearby prep school and enjoyed the task thanks to the resourcefulness of many of the candidates.

A random sample showed that the owner of *The Times* is called "Murderdoch", the author of the Iliad was one F. F. Forsyth and the last book of the Bible is Revolution. Furthermore, a chihuahua is apparently a type of chinese curry, Richard Branson is a pickle manufacturer and W. G. Grace was associated with ballet (reasonable enough, when you think about it).

To cap it all, in answer to the question, "where was Saul going when struck blind?", one boy wrote, "fishing".

Peterborough Column of the Daily Telegraph

September of '33. I took a bugle with me that had been a gift from some friend of my parents who had presumably played it in the first World War. It seemed a very logical thing to do. I'd been told that in schools they taught you how to do things and, as no-one at home seemed to be prepared to tell me how to play the bugle, I was sure I would get the necessary guidance now that I was entering an establishment that actually specialised in teaching. But, no such luck. Kindergarten teachers were not only unwilling to teach me how to play the bugle, they were not too thrilled about having the instrument in their classroom, and I was instructed to take 'that thing' home at the end of the day and leave it there.

I didn't learn how to play the trombone when I was eight years old even though my father would insist that I go upstairs to practise every evening after dinner. Perhaps I didn't learn because he would also insist that I stop after about five minutes as unendurable trombone noises cascaded downstairs into his study. Some years later when I went away to the New Mexico Military Institute, I didn't learn how to play the clarinet, although the bandmaster, Captain Ted Hunt, made a very determined try at teaching me. I think this is where it first began to dawn on me that the freedom to pursue one's goals in the world does not necessarily mean success.

It was at new Mexico that I also learned a great deal about discipline, integrity and honour. Not that I was without any knowledge of these concepts before I got to the school, but abstract concepts were brought kicking and screaming into the real world, my real world, in my first boarding school days. I went to New Mexico in 1942, during the War, as my parents started to think in terms of my ultimately serving in the US Army. I was already fourteen years old and the War didn't look like it was coming to a speedy conclusion.

Nevertheless, NMMI made a different person of me than I might otherwise have been. A good school certainly has a dramatic effect on your personality and character, and I like to think that my cavalry school days enhanced mine. At any rate, I have a much clearer recollection of the teachers and administrative officers there than I did of any of my instructors in my

grammar school days in Buffalo, Junior High School days in Florida, and even in the seven later years that I spent at the University of Chicago.

I failed Latin the first year that I took it in Florida. When I got to New Mexico, where they made us study every night after dinner until taps, my academic status changed. Not only was I first in my class in Latin, but in my first year at NMMI, where they posted the grades for all to see every month, I led my class and, consequently, won the class scholarship.

It was during my second year there that I came as near as ever to being kicked out of any school. At the time I was the roommate of Nicky Hilton, Conrad Hilton Jr, the son of the famous hotelier. I had chosen Nicky as a roommate because I noticed that on his desk he had a picture of a very beautiful blonde lady. This was a subject that was beginning to interest me a great deal and I figured that anybody that knew anyone that good looking could be a source of great help and guidance to a neophyte in the field.

'Just how do you go about getting a great looking girl friend like that?', I finally asked. 'How the hell should I know,' replied Nicky, 'that's my stepmother, Zsa Zsa Gabor'.

Nevertheless, forgetting the sophisticated guidance for which I thought I was going to be in line, my friendship with Nicky carried on and we remained good friends to the end of his days. This was true even though Nicky's next roommate represented a rather big improvement over the palsy-walsy days of NMMI. Fresh out of military school, Nicky married Elizabeth Taylor but, then, that roommate situation didn't last too long either.

As his Dad owned a hotel in El Paso, Texas, Nicky was sometimes allowed to go and visit him on weekends when it didn't conflict with major events in the school programme. From one of these expeditions Nicky returned to school with a dozen miniature, eighth-of-a-pint, bottles of whisky. This was strictly against school rules – being caught drinking meant immediate expulsion.

Actually, Nicky intended to use the bottles as a sort of decorative touch in our room. I pointed out to him that this would never stand up to inspection and that we'd all get booted out of NMMI. Therefore, we decided the easiest solution to the problem was to empty the contents as quickly as possible in the most convenient receptacle around – down our throats.

This may all seem a bit silly in retrospect, but in those days the idea of doing anything so daring as having an actual drink of real whisky was the kind of rebellious invention that particularly appeals to sixteen and seventeen year-olds locked up in a military academy.

There were about twelve of these little bottles and there were five of us lads in the room, and we started mixing up the drinks with Coca Cola and water, playing records and having a hell of a good time.

As we finished off each little bottle Jack Howard would lean out the back

---

Q How did Wellington manage to defeat a much larger French Army in the Peninsular War?
A The French had a much larger army, so there was more to hit.

window of the room, and deftly toss the empty bottle up on the flat roof over our heads. The idea of using them for decoration had been totally abandoned.

At some point in the proceedings I needed to leave the room to saunter down the balcony to the men's lavatory that served the rooms on our floor of the barracks. While I was out of the room a tactical officer walked by the window of our room and saw what was going on. He immediately spotted the small social gathering, which itself was a bit out of the ordinary, and the tiny bottles on the desk were not to be ignored.

Major Stapp – that was the officer's name – strode into the room and started taking down names to report to the Commandant.

While all this was going on I came back from the washroom and, fortunately, looked in through the window and saw the disaster that was occurring. Four cadets standing at rigid attention, and a tactical officer with one of those Texas-Ranger-like campaign hats writing furiously in his dreaded notebook.

Immediately, I thought better of rejoining the festivities, and headed off for the school gymnasium to think things out and decide what the best course of action might be.

'Boy, were you lucky you weren't in the room, Stapp came in – we're all busted for drinking and this could be the end', said Nicky when I ventured back after a safe interval. 'Apparently he saw Jack throwing the bottles up on the roof', continued Nicky, referring to the work of our bottle disposal expert, who we thought had gone totally unobserved.

'Lucky Lownes,' Jack Howard said, 'You sure lead a charmed life. This is the first time I've ever heard of anyone being saved by a flush outside of a poker game. I wish to hell I had felt the urge', he added.

My first reaction to all of this was the feeling of a lucky escape. The others looked pretty forlorn with the exception of Nicky who had begun to focus on the positive aspects of life outside the Institute.

'As soon as we get out,' Nicky tried to cheer up the others, 'We'll head down to El Paso, check into the Hilton Hotel, and I'll show you one hell of a time over in Jaurez.' Just across the bridge over the Rio Grande was the wide open Mexican town that Nicky began describing as singularly dedicated to consoling cadets – rather ex-cadets – from NMMI.

'You ain't going to miss Captain Dwight H. H. Starr's Spanish class when you meet the señoritas that hold up the bar in the bodega where I bought those miniatures,' the small bottles that had been confiscated by Major Stapp for evidence.

Nicky put a record on, upbeat Latin American music, *Guantanamera,* and started punctuating his description of the lurid delights of Jaurez, with handclapping and flamenco-style heel stomping. The atmosphere in the room changed. The four 'doomed' cadets, beamed at Nick Hilton's detailed description of the high life across the border unfettered by wartime USA rationing and shortages and New Mexico Military Institute discipline.

There was still just enough alcohol in their systems to forestall any consideration of the consequences of expulsion to their scholastic records, military ambitions and family relations. Nobody seemed to be too concerned either about where the dinero was coming from to finance the new hedonistic lifestyle with the rhumba beat.

The only really depressed cadet in that room was me. The lucky guy who happened to be out of the trench when the mortar shell landed. Not only would I miss out on all the planned fun but I'd be stuck here alone at full attention in regimental uniform spit and polish with my four best friends gone away. Gone away to indescribable pleasures and adventures 'south-of-the-border – down Mexico way', as the song has it.

That night, after taps, was the first time I had trouble getting to sleep in two years at the Institute. The alcohol had worn off so I wasn't tormented with the missed promise of El Paso and Jaurez high-jinks. Instead I started to think of the unfairness of the real situation. Four scholastic careers interrupted and permanently tarnished but one, mine, spared for an almost silly reason – I had to go pee at the right moment.

What would my four friends think of 'lucky' me as they packed up to leave the Institute? What would I think about myself? I'd miss the others for sure but that wasn't enough. They were going to be expelled for doing wrong but I'd been just as wrong and I was going to go unpunished. What would other cadets think about the whole drama and what would they think about the one that got away with it all? I decided what I would do and fell asleep.

Next morning at regimental formation the names of cadets 'on report' were read out. After breakfast the reported cadets would line up outside the Commandant's office. As each one came out, the next would step into the office, snap to attention, salute the Commandant, Colonel Saunders, and state his name 'answering report.'

Colonel Saunders would read off the reported transgression from the book in front of him. The cadet would 'accept' or 'challenge' the report and provide any explanation that might modify the verdict and the punishment that Colonel Saunders would immediately decree, loss of privileges, extra duties, confinement to barracks – that sort of thing.

That sort of thing – unless something really serious was going to result in the demotion of a cadet officer or, for a real humdinger like drinking or going AWOL, expulsion. In all those cases Colonel Saunders would dismiss the cadet, telling him, 'Your penalty will be announced at this evening's roll call'. One never wanted to hear those words, they meant disaster.

And those were just the words that Nick Hilton said he heard after he and the others had answered their reports. I told him that I was going to go straight into Saunder's office, and tell him my part in the escapade.

I didn't want to seem the martyr so I just playfully punched Nick on the arm and said that I'd be damned if I was going to miss out on all the fun and excitement he and the others were going to be having.

'Private First Class Lownes, V.L. reporting, Sir!"

'I don't seem to see your name on my report list, Lownes,' Colonel Saunders scanned the opened book.

'Alcoholic beverage in possession. Whether it's in the book or not, Sir.'

'Lownes, are you saying that you were involved with Hilton, Howard, Haldiman and Vibert?'

'Sir, I'm not only saying I was involed but it was my suggestion that got them all into this trouble. Nick Hilton bought those miniatures just to decorate the room. It was my bright idea to drink the contents – the empty bottles wouldn't be so likely to cause us trouble, Sir.'

'Lownes, if you were going to drink the contents and use the bottles for decoration, why was Howard throwing the empty bottles up on the roof; or was it the roof you were going to decorate?'

'Sir, after we emptied the bottles we could see they wouldn't be very decorative and we were afraid that someone in authority might just ask us where the contents had gone. The bottles looked just as dangerous empty as they had full. Maybe more so, Sir.'

'Lownes, where were you when Major Stapp caught the others? Hiding in the locker or under the bed?'

'Of course not, Sir. If I had been hiding, Sir, I wouldn't likely be here now. The fact is, Sir, I went to the john. I saw Major Stapp in the room when I came back so I just kept on walking.'

'I see, Lownes,' Saunders paused and then fixed me with his most serious look, downright grim. 'You do realize that, even though you're reporting yourself, you will receive the same punishment the others are getting?'

'Yes, Sir.'

Saunders shook his head and snapped out the dreaded closing line, 'Your penalty will be announced at this evening's roll call. Cadet PFC Lownes, dismissed.'

I saluted, did a smart about-face and marched out, resigned to being expelled but rather proud of myself for doing the right thing.

The regiment formed up for the evening roll call. Special announcements were read out over the loudspeaker by the Officer of the Day. The names of the culprits who had been found breaking rules or failing to be sufficiently punctual or sufficiently tidy were read out. Each name was followed by a brief description of the transgression, for example, lights on after taps, and then a recitation of the punishment – confined to barracks for two weekends or whatever.

When the name Haldiman, J. R. came up on the alphabetically arranged list, I drew a deep breath. All of us would get what John received. Immediate expulsion? No! I couldn't believe my ears.

'Haldiman, J. R., alcoholic beverages in possession; seventy-five demerits and seventy-five tours.'

I resisted the urge to throw up my cap in the air and let out a very unmilitary cheer. Such behaviour would only bring another report and more punishment. Besides, maybe there was some special reason Haldiman was getting off lightly. The rest of us might get the standard drinks treatment? By-bye NMMI?

We didn't have to wait long to find out. Hilton, C. N. was next on the list and Howard, J. B. right after Hilton. Same for Hilton, same for Howard. Then, ditto Lownes and ditto Vibert.

Seventy-five demerits, that would confine us to campus for the rest of the school year. Only three months to go, thank God. And, as for the seventy-five tours, than meant walking with a rifle and a full pack one hundred and fifty miles around a two hundred foot square walkway in the centre of the barracks area.

Finding time on a crowded schedule to walk off the tours was difficult but we would all have to do it, an hour or two at a time.

Did the others figure that my turning myself in saved their butts from getting kicked out of the Institute? Did my, ahem, very military and courageous honesty make the authorities look for an excuse to go easy on five cadets whose total alcohol consumption wouldn't have intoxicated a thirsty owl?

Did I receive proper recognition for my noble deed from my four buddies whose academic careers I might very well have saved?

Well, I'll let one of the others answer that question. Jack Howard came up to me after we both had been walking off tours with full pack under a hot New Mexico sun for about three hours on a Saturday afternoon. Jack looked at me across the watercooler, wiped the back of his hand across a sweaty forehead and, doubtless thinking of the many more hours of this agony we would have to endure, said, 'Lownes, you son-of-a-bitch, if it weren't for you I could be sitting right now, in an air conditioned bar in Jaurez drinking Margaritas with, maybe, Margarita herself. Thanks a lot.'

Victor Lownes

My war

Upon returning to Eton I quickly joined the Royal Observer Corps and additionally became an ARP messenger. This latter post had distinct advantages, as I found out during the summer term of 1944 when flying bombs were dropping all round Windsor and Slough. About twice a week, I was detailed to sleep alone in the ARP Headquarters in the Eton Town Hall. I was told that when the siren went off above my head, I was to don my ARP uniform and take a message somewhere. Alas, I was never called to do so. The greatest privilege in wartime Eton was that ARP messengers were

134

allowed bicycles at all times, which made getting to classes on time much easier. Of course, when a siren did go at night, the whole school decamped into the house shelters, which entailed the cancelling of 'Early School', that uncivilised Eton practice of a whole class period before breakfast.

Another wartime experience at Eton was war work on Sundays, mostly cleaning up scrap at factories in Slough and, best of all, fire watching, when a group of our 17-year-old boys, just prior to joining up, were asked to report to school during the summer holidays of 1944 and take shifts sitting on the roofs of various buildings in case of incendiary attacks. Here we were at school with almost complete freedom, virtually no discipline, no work, no school uniform. We could go where and when we liked, visit pubs and enjoy ourselves. I never spotted a fire but I did have a memorable time.

Lord Montagu of Beaulieu

All for love

The idea of raising money by means of ransom did not begin or end the story of Richard Coeur-de-Lion. In World War II, as in most other wars, those at home collected cash for those who fought overseas. At our boarding school in 1942 there was a campaign to raise money for the Merchant Navy. In different ways we were all expected to join in.

In the isolated seaside community to which we had been evacuated there was one heavenly, beautiful and aloof girl who fortnightly appeared at weekends. It was said she was a nurse at some distant hospital and that she was related to the owners of the cottage where she stayed though the owners were seldom there. Our secret plan was to kidnap her and hold her ransom. Every boy in the school was in love with her – every boy would donate all his pocket money to the Merchant Navy to obtain her release.

A great deal of thought went into the operation. There was an empty hotel in a wood on the far side of the bay – here we prepared for her a dungeon with a small store of food – we were reckoning on a short overnight imprisonment and a release on Sunday afternoon. The coup was planned to take place on a very dark Saturday night.

The black-out always provided us with virtually unlimited scope for 'breaking-out'. Because of the risk and memory of air-raids no doors were ever locked. On previous sorties we had plotted her movements – she usually arrived by the last train. We would let her have supper, ring the front door bell and then capture her in an enormous sack which we had acquired for the purpose.

One of the most formidable members of the school's academic staff was Douglas Fox. A supremely gifted musician, he had lost an arm on the Western front in World War I and taught with an agressive brilliance that partly stemmed from pain and his frustration. We were not aware that without warning that afternoon he had changed his lodgings. When he answered our knock at the front door in the near-total darkness which the black-out regulations demanded, long before we could distinguish our victim, he was a prisoner in our sack.

What were we to do? Not a boy would contribute one penny to procure the release of so fearsome an adversary. In his sack, which by now was firmly tied at the neck, he writhed like a monstrous eel. In those days we had not seen the opera 'Rigoletto' or else we might have hit upon a quick solution to our problem; instead, we just ran.

It was rather fortunate that the name of our 'house' began with the letter W. Fox fought his way out of the sack and telephoned all the housemasters in turn but by the time our housemaster was alerted we were feigning sleep in our beds.

Never again did we catch sight of our divinely beautiful would-be captive, but a rumour went round some weeks later that she had gone off and married someone in the Merchant Navy.

Rodney Exton

Picric papers

This story begins with a bang and may end with a bang. The first explosion occurred through my discovering, at the age of eleven, the process for making gunpowder. The recipe can be found – or could in those days be found – in the *Encyclopaedia Brittanica*. All you need is saltpetre, charcoal, and rock sulphur in the proportions 75:15:10, and you get a powder the colour of a grey flannel suit but tinted a faint yellow by the sulphur. I also learned that if you prepare a cardboard cone, and ram the mixture into the cone so that it is tightly packed and sealed, and you include a fuse of string soaked in a saltpetre solution, and light it with a match, you can create a very satisfying bang. Equally satisfying to the junior pryomaniac is the Guy Fawkes smell of combusted chemicals, a musty-sweet and sulphurous aroma with a special character all of its own.

Unable to foresee the consequences, my father indulgently bought me a chemistry set from the Houndsditch Warehouse, and I started experimenting. The chemistry lab at school, although well stocked with all manner of goodies, was well-protected from inquisitive little fingers and every gramme had to be accounted for since it was rumoured that one boy had blown himself up while trying the make mercury fulminate. Surprisingly, rule-of-thumb recipes for these lethal compounds can be found in many reference libraries, and in the 1940s you could walk into a pharmacy and buy most of the ingredients over the counter.

In the cellar of our home, and during the school holidays, I had a bash at making nitro-glycerine. 'NG' as it is known in the trade, was not invented (as I had thought) by Alfred Nobel, but by someone called Sobrero, in 1846, and is produced by the action of nitric and sulphuric acids on glycerine. It goes off with an awesome bang . . . From the pharmacy I purchased the acids, and a bottle of medicinal glycerine. I must have been mad. NG is notoriously unstable, but I managed to make a slightly oily, colourless fluid, and in sufficient quantity to lift the roof off. Did I really make nitro-glycerine? I rang the Nobel Explosives Division of ICI to ask. 'If you had done,' they said, 'you'd have known about it.'

Perhaps I was lucky. I followed Nobel's technique of making the explosive inert by mixing it with Fuller's earth, the recipe for dynamite. I packed the stuff in a tin and for all I know that tin is still there, in the cellar of a house in West Kensington, where I left it when we moved. In my view, explosions were the natural outcome of chemistry experiments. Watching litmus paper turn blue, or making solutions form crystals was all fairly boring, unless the crystals happened to be ammonium iodide, an extremely delicate and combustible mixture.

The ingredients were simple – idoine crystals dissolved in ammonia; you pour the solution on to blotting paper and crystals reform when the solution dries out. When you touch the crystals with the point of a pencil, they explode with a sharp *crack!* Schoolmasters and parents proved inordinately critical of my achievements when the classrooms echoed with the crackle of explosions like musketry, and I later confined my experiments to the relative safety of our home. I stress 'relative safety' since a flying bomb landed in our back garden and blew me out of bed. My ears sang for a week. I lurched into the dining room, where my father was having breakfast. He remained seated at the table, with shards of glass embedded in his neck, finishing his toast. He was a veteran of the first World War. 'Bloody Boche,' he growled. We were obliged to move in with relatives, while the house was made habitable again.

In a room which my father used as an office I mixed equal quantities of the two chemicals in a cocoa tin, placed the tin on a metal tripod, and pushed a lighted candle underneath. By this action I was possibly certifiable. A thin and evil wisp of smoke ascended from the tin. It looked somehow sinister. I retreated, and was halfway out of the house when there was a stupendous bang out of all proportion to the modest quantity of chemicals. The house shook. Somewhere a pane of glass came adrift from a window frame. The curtains were ablaze. The experiment was successful, but my parent's reaction was equally violent. I was given to understand, forcibly, that Baird & Tatlock and the chemists of Greater London would have to survive without my regular custom. I was to confine my experiments to a tranquil pursuit.

'Can't you do something that we'd *all* appreciate,' pleaded my mother, 'like making a cake, or something?'

I went into the kitchen and mixed margarine, sugar, dried eggs, flour, cocoa, and a few drops of vanilla essence to make a chocolate cake. It rose rather splendidly. I covered the cake with icing, and family and friends fell upon it unashamedly. It was, remember, towards the end of the war, and the ingredients represented the combined rations of several people – but the experiment was a success. Where ingredients permitted I began to work my way through my mother's recipe books. And that, I suppose, is how I became a cook.

Adrian Bailey

Half in and Half out of Uniform

The CCF in World War II was in many instances merged with the local Home Guard. Older boys awaiting their call-up papers to join the forces were old enough to be fully fledged members of official Home Guard units, those in the age group below joined something known as the Junior Home Guard. Most schools had three uniform parades per week, in addition not infrequently to nocturnal fire-watching and stirrup-pump drill to combat the incendiary bombs which seldom fell. The energy put into these endless parades and rehearsals was not matched by opportunities to put theory into practice. The consequence was a growing sense of restlessness.

In the summer of 1942 a chance came to end the frustration, there was to be a "Mock Invasion" – our school Home Guard detachment would be involved. The élite section of the unit called itself the "Commando" and its forte was cliff-climbing, a skill which it incessantly practised for reasons of its own. When it received its Mock Invasion orders from headquarters the "Commando" was mortified to learn that its task was to dig latrines.

Those of us who were not of a warlike nature foresaw the Mock Invasion in an entirely different light. The nearest girls boarding school, into whose high-walled confines no boy had ever set foot, was designated as a casualty clearing station. By means of faked concussion on the eve of the Mock Invasion, contrived in public view at high jump training, I succeeded in being put "off parade" and in being selected as a civilian casualty, spending the afternoon being bandaged and unbandaged by a sequence of delightful schoolgirls. The "Commando" meanwhile was fed up with lavatory duties and, in defiance of orders from above, set off at nightfall along the beach with the aim of climbing the cliffs to win our local make-believe war by taking the enemy in the rear.

It was on the following morning, as I was returning to my stretcher in anticipation of a day of further bandages and more cups of hot tea being nervously spilt down my open shirt, when the "Commando" returned in disgrace. Exhausted by their midnight march along the sand and their ascent of a vertical cliff they had fallen asleep and been captured without, so to speak, firing a shot. Their trousers came back by parcel post a few days later.

Rodney Exton

Religious knowledge and lack of it

A form of prayer

The headmaster barked an order and in we went, like mice beneath his hawkish nose and eye, the bristling ginger moustache, the sharp jaw. Heads down, staring at his checked plus-fours for which we were quickly to discover an unrepeatable name, we filed into our classrooms.

'Good morning, boys and girls.'

'Good morning, Miss McNeil.'

'All stand. Our Father . . .'

> *Which art in heffen*
> *Hallo pee thigh name*
> *Thigh kinktom come*
> *Thigh will pee ton*
> *On earth is it ish in heffen*
> *Giff us this tay our taily prett*
> *Ant forgiff us our tetts*
> *As wee forgiff our tettors*
> *Ant leet us not into temptation*
> *Putt teliffer us from eefill*
> *For thighn ish the kinktom*
> *Ant the power ant the clory*
> *Foreffer*
> *Amen*

'Amen.'

Miss McNeil. Highland Miss McNeil. Amen for Highland Mary.

Laurie Lee

Grace forgot

Grace was said before every meal, by the most senior member of the house present.

On one particular occasion, whoever was due to say grace suddenly forgot the words! Panic struck, he turned and delegated the task to the boy next to him. Unfortunately, he too was promptly struck dumb; and, in desperation, dug me in the ribs, indicating that it was my turn.

Boldly, I intoned: 'For what we are about to receive . . .' only to be halted temporarily in mid-sentence by a delayed attack of the same amnesia! Undeterred, I racked my brain, and blurted out the only liturgical phrase I could remember: 'Good Lord, deliver us!'

Andrew M. Williamson

The bibles in churches are very heavy, so they are usually held in a rectum which is usually made of oak, carved like an eagle.

Silent prayer

Religion a form of social control? Assembly starts with a prayer after the school has filed silently into the hall. Usually the prayer followed naturally enough, but occasionally the children were not quite as silent as they should be . . . Headmaster: 'Let us pray . . . and that means SHUT UP!'

The **Australian**

Church courts in mediaeval times held no terror for the wayward priest: 'It was easier for priests; all they got was a few prayers to say and Bloody Marys.'

STORIES OUT OF SCHOOL

Prayers at public school

Attendance at divine service was exacted as a gesture of obedience and acknowledgement of orthodoxy. It was an obligatory 'Church parade' and was treated as such by the boys. Their conduct during services was at times 'abominable'. The boys had no prayer books and did not know the words of the psalms. When their lips moved they were making social communications in song to their neighbours. On 8 May 1824, we have Milnes Gaskell writing to his mother, 'A clergyman read prayers for about 20 minutes but was perfectly inaudible on account of the noise made by the boys.'

John Chandos

Ear tests

Certain boys, instead of abandoning interest entirely, treated inaudibility as a challenge, and competed and collaborated to extort some sense from the effusion. Some shut their eyes tight (the better to hear), others opened them wide and fixed them on the mouth of the speaker in the hope of reading from his lips what they could not receive from his speech. There was an occasion when one experienced and conscientious player of this game, although he strained all his faculties, could only make out one word of an entire sermon, and that sounded like 'shoe-strings'. He did distinctly hear that word three times, but was unable to establish any context whatever.

One of the most conscientious of the sermon tasters was William Gladstone and his frustrations are recorded in his diary.

Sunday, October 9th, 1825. Plumptre preached on lying . . .
Saturday October 16th. Plumptre preached . . . could hardly hear.
Sunday 4th December, Sermon from the Vice Provost – Prepare ye the way of the Lord. Very little of it audible.

How little and how slowly things changed at Eton may be judged by the perpetuation up to and beyond the halfway mark of the century of this orthodoxy of clerical obscurantism. Goodford was a boy at school with

---

After telling my class the Easter story one eight-year-old boy, who had been listening with great attention said,
'Isn't that shocking Miss?'
'Isn't what shocking Paul?' I replied.
'That Judas should sell Jesus for thirty pieces of silver.'
'It certainly is', I agreed, delighted that the story had such a profound effect.
'Yes,' he continued, 'he could have got at least a hundred.'

Morning prayer
This morning let us pray that the trouble between the Arabs and the Israelis can be settled in a true Christian manner.

Gladstone. Later, when as Provost he read prayers, only one word, Wuffaw (wherefore) was generally intelligible. Whenever in the conduct of a service, Wuffaw was heard more than once, an audible groan went up, for it meant that he had strayed back to the beginning of the prayer. Goodford's voice was a distinctive mixture of a languid Cambridge drawl and a residual West Country burr. On a memorable occasion he preached on the text 'Remember Lot's Wife'. That was about all that was heard, but Lot's wife was remembered, and in after years Old Etonians who had been present could give exact imitations of the sounds, if not the import, of the peroration.

John Chandos

Shirking Chapel

Thurs. May 25th, 1820: 'Sat up all night with 3 other fellows swigging wine and playing cards. We had 3 bottles and a fine ham. Shirked chapel next morning. We had about 2 hours' sleep and I was told I looked very unwell next morning, I felt very sleepy. Meredith was much worse than I; after breakfast I was very well.'

Sat. 27th: 'All our room overslept themselves, so we shirked chapel, got off the roll being shirked down.'

Minet's Journal, 1818–20

Grace Abounding

Most young children of my generation learned their prayers at their mother's knee long before they had learned to read. This could lead to problems. An extremely intelligent and articulate Irish actress of my acquaintance told me that until her early teens she had faithfully recited the rosary every night at school repeating "Hail Mary, full of *grapes,* the Lord is with thee . . ." etc. As the age of reason came upon her with its consequent puzzlements, she had been forced to design for herself a whole new theology along the lines – Grapes = Wine; bread and wine = communion etc. It was only at the age of 17 when, having become "Head Girl" at her convent school one of her

---

The vicar asked the class how many boys and girls would like to go to Heaven. Only one little girl kept her hand down. When the vicar asked her why she replied. 'Me mum said I had to go straight home.'

The Good Samaritan
'Why did the priest and Levi pass by on the other side?'
   'Because they would have seen that the man had already been robbed.'

Tell, in your own words, the story of a Parable.
'This man went out to sew seeds. Some of these seeds fell on nice ground and some fell on stones. Which only goes to show that you have to watch what you are doing when you are sewing seeds.'

---

duties was to read morning prayers. She saw the 'Ave' in print for the first time and was forced to a cataclysmic re-consideration of her religious position. It was grace, not grapes.

Garrett Anderson

Comprehension

In the '50s, Irish National Schools were very strictly run with regular tests for the children and frequent, but unexpected, checks on the teachers themselves by visiting Inspectors.

One of my friends was setting an English Comprehension test for her class of eight-year-olds. In this they were given various nouns which they had to use in a complete sentence to demonstrate that they knew their meaning. One of the words she chose on this occasion was 'NUN'.

That night, marking the papers, my friend found that one little boy had written, 'A nun is a lady in confinement', to which, being in skittish mood, she appended her own comment, 'A strange conception'.

As ill-luck would have it, the following morning there came an Inspector of particularly stern and Savanarola-like aspect who collected her own and her children's work for examination. Nervously she went on with the class, fully expecting her career to be at an end, while the Inspector sat grimly at the back, occasionally listening, occasionally flipping through the written exercises he had taken from her desk.

Nothing was said, however, and at the end of the period the Inspector handed back her papers and left with a courteous bow. Thinking that, by a miracle, he had missed her offending piece of levity, she riffled through the papers to find it and remove it forever. There it was: 'A nun is a lady in confinement' and her own comment, 'a strange conception'; only now there had been added, in precise copperplate, 'obviously a clerical error.'

Garrett Anderson

Religion under Keate

A notorious incident centred upon the person of a celebrated tenor, John Hobbs. The voluntary had ended. The congregation rose and the instrumental introduction to Handel's *Messiah* was played. All waited with silent attention for the opening notes of the voice. 'Co-o-mfort ye, my people' rose in thrilling tones into the air; again and again the noble phrase

---

Kate (aged 6) writing about the Nativity noted that 'Elizabeth, Mary's cousin had a baby too, and she called him John the Basket'.

Anne Robson

was repeated, and a fourth time it was being sustained to a climax, when the exquisite sounds were distorted into a shriek of agony. Amidst subdued commotion, John Hobbs was seen to be assisted, limping and moaning, from the chapel by solicitous attendants. It was supposed that the great man had suffered a fit; but what had happened was that, as he reached his top note for the fourth time, one of the confirmation candidates had driven a pin into the calf of his leg. It is not unlikely that the perpetrator became a clergyman, perhaps even a prelate, for Eton, during Keate's time, produced above its average of bishops.

John Chandos

The £500 sermon

B. L. Balfour, unaffectionately known as 'The Bulb', was one of those sixth-formers who was held in high esteem by juniors but regarded as an absolute menace by the academic staff.

'The Bulb' was having a bad term. He had made a book on the school cross-country race and lost heavily when the favourite won. His insurance scheme, which provided financial compensation for the victim of corporal punishment, added to his losses when the headmaster, normally a mild man, instituted mass canings as a reprisal for general misbehaviour on Founder's Day. 'The Bulb' paid up with a plump and greasy smile – but behind the grimace was the fear of having to account to father at the end of term. Somehow he must recoup his losses – but how?

An opportunity came unexpectedly. On two successive Sundays a different visiting preacher had begun his sermon with the words 'What is man?', quoting from a context in the *Psalms*. On the second occasion boys had to duck down below the pews stuffing handkerchiefs in their mouths to stop themselves from laughing out loud. Virtually every word of the second sermon was identical with the first: man was 50 per cent water, 2 per cent calcium, 1 per cent iron etc. or something like that. Quite obviously both preachers were using the same copy. It was a chance in a thousand – or was it?

Almost before the school had giggled its way out of the chapel 'The Bulb' was laying odds of 100-to-1 that the visiting preacher the following Sunday would not perform the hat-trick. The bets poured in.

By Saturday 'The Bulb' began to get worried. He had taken £5, mostly in pennies, to win £500. School fees in those days were about £200 per annum so the amounts were relatively colossal. He was worried because a boy had received a letter from his brother at another boarding school which included comments about his school chaplain's obsession with 'Man' and it was this very chaplain who would be coming over to preach the next Sunday. 'The Bulb' was short of options, he could not lay off the bets. The impossible sequence of three in a row suddenly seemed a probability.

There was only one hope. The visiting chaplain would arrive on the Saturday evening and he would be travelling by rail. 'The Bulb' would cunningly find out which train he was coming on and would join it several stations along the line. The chaplain would be wearing his dog-collar. 'The Bulb' would recognise him and ask him about his sermon. If the text were to be 'What is man?' he would convince the preacher with immense courtesy that he would be wise to choose some alternative in view of what had already occurred on the two previous Sundays.

So 'The Bulb' feigned a knee injury on the Saturday morning and he was put off games. He found out the preacher's expected time of arrival and sloped away to catch the down-train on which the preacher would be travelling. 'The Bulb's' plan was sound but, unknown to him, the preacher had already missed a connection and he now was aiming to arrive on Sunday just in time for the chapel. 'The Bulb' went from end to end of an empty train and returned in despair.

Next morning when the preacher climbed up into the pulpit the school congregation was on tenterhooks. It was as if a hanging judge was about to pronounce sentence. 'For my sermon this morning I choose as my theme the question "What is . . ."' – gasps of interruption from the congregation . . . . The preacher began again. 'I choose as my theme the question "What is m . . ?"' – more gasps . . . . "What is meant by the word Charity?"' There was a sigh from the back of the chapel and a crash – 'The Bulb' had fainted.

Rodney Exton

Parents

Please repeat that

A boy from a split home, living with father, was dropped off at school in the morning as usual by his mother. Being more disinclined to attend school than usual he walked round the corner to the nearest public telephone.

Phoning the school he said,

'This is Mr Brown here, I am afraid John is ill and will be unable to attend school today.'

'OK', said the secretary, 'what form is you son in, Mr Brown?'

'I'm in 5B!', came the reply.

He always did wonder how the headmaster found out!

R. D. W. Rhodes

One's parents

I was presently elected to the Political Society. This used to meet in the Provost and Vice Provost's rooms to entertain some distinguished guest. I remember, in particular, a . . . James Maxton, the Clydeside leader of the Independent Labour party . . . He began his talk by saying, 'I don't know how many of your parents have been to prison.' This was good shock tactics and gripped our attention at once. 'I suspect many of them deserved to, but few did,' he went on. 'This is a pity because no man's education is complete until he's done a spell inside.'

Julian Amery

Dr Vaughan of Harrow

To a self-important mother who said that before she entered her son for the school she must ask the headmaster whether he was particular about the social antecedents of the boys accepted, he is said to have replied, 'Dear Madam, as long as your son behaves himself and his fees are paid no questions will be asked about his social antecedents.'

John Chandos

Learning lost

During my schooldays my future was always uncertain. The Boy, what will he become? was a question that received a different answer almost daily. My brother Avmine had got a scholarship and gone to Oxford, and the idea was that, if I got a scholarship too, I would join him there. All through my last term at Dulwich, I sprang from my bed at five sharp each morning, ate a couple of petit beurre biscuits and worked like a beaver at my Homer and

Thucylides, but just as scholarship time was approaching, with me full to the brim with classic lore and just spoiling for a good whack at the examiners, the rupee starting creating again, and it seemed to my father that two sons at the University would be a son more than the privy purse could handle. So learning drew the loser's end and commerce got me.

P. G. Wodehouse

Ignorance is bliss

My cousin Nigel Lawson's seven-year-old son was duly sent off to his prep school. A quiet, thinking child, who had had several conversations with his housemaster, a charming young man, before it occurred to Dominic that his housemaster's name was the same as that of the headmaster. After some thought on the subject, and at their next meeting, he decided to mention the fact. 'Sir,' he said, 'your name is the same as the headmaster, why?'

'Well,' came the reply, 'I am his son.' No comment came from the child so he explained further 'The headmaster is my father you see.'

'Oh,' said Dominic, 'really.' Then after more thought, 'Did you know that when you took on the job?'

Libby Hess

Writing home to mother
Dear Mother,
    Please write soon even if it is only two or three pounds.
        Love, Clint

The little girl saying to her governess, 'Me slept wiv Daddy last night, Miss Jones.' 'That's not right, dear,' answers Miss Jones. '*I* slept with Daddy!' The expressions on the faces of the little girl's mother and father indicate that this is an idea which had occurred to them both, though with different feelings.

The classroom door was flung open and there stood Bill's father complaining that the teacher had thumped little Bill. The teacher said that all the details were in the staffroom and he would fetch them and asked Bill's father to 'Keep this lot quiet until I get back.' He went to the staffroom for the punishment book, made a cup of tea, lit a cigarette, drank the tea and waited for the sound to grow in volume as the class began to erupt. At the critical time the teacher moved back down the corridor to be met by Bill's father shouting, 'Here, mate, thump the bloody lot!'

Dear Teacher,
    I have seen in the paper that you want to know if you can punish children. You can punish mine as I am in favour of discipline and capital punishment for children as it never did me any harm.
        Thank you.

Father's wishes

A sturdy child, broad for his years, he seemed bursting with life and health, and, even at this early age, with intellectual curiosity. He never stopped asking questions, that wonderful form of self-education which intelligent children evolve for themselves. The questions were, naturally, on every subject within his range – or, as for that, outside; there was no sign of specialisation, or of the direction in which his interests would lie when he was older. But I remember that when a friend of the family's, for something to say, asked him what he would be when he grew up, he shifted the responsibility by replying, "*My father* wishes me to be an engine-driver."

Osbert Sitwell

One-upmanship

Child 1. 'In the holidays, we're going to stay with friends in a castle'
Child 2. 'We live in a castle'

Peter King

Child 1. 'I told the chauffeur to take off his cap, in case the other girls thought me a snob'
Child 2. 'Our chauffeur always wears his cap. It would be so awful if anyone thought he was Daddy'

Jilly Cooper

Parental priorities

It was commonplace for a father to profess, 'He will be satisfied if his son never does anything unworthy of a gentleman.'

John Chandos

Irish profundity

'Bulls' are a form of humour peculiar to the Irish and all the funnier, often, for being quite unconscious. 'A person couldn't be in two places at once – barring he was a bird' is a typical sample from the eighteenth-century Irish M.P., Sir Boyle Roche who was famous for many similar profundities.

When I was about twelve and had just completed my common entrance examination, my old aunt came up from Sligo for the day as a gesture of support and to take me out to tea. Seizing my examination paper from my hand she eyed it scornfully for a moment and at once came out with a classic example: 'If you fail that, me bucko,' she declared, 'you don't deserve to pass.'

Garrett Anderson

Changing the subject

The first of my four sons, Nigel, was in the summer term of his first year at Stowe. As an Old Stoic, I had taken my wife, my mother and my three younger sons up for Speech Day. It was a hot day and we had a picnic down by the lakes. The boys were in and out of the mud at the water's edge. They did not enjoy being cleaned up for the formal speeches and house tea afterwards. Eventually, all were packed into the car to go up to the main school – reasonably spruce and definitely resenting the 'waste' of a fine afternoon. The youngest, James, was extremely rude to my wife. She decided that, on this occasion, discretion was the better part of something and that ignoring him would be best for all concerned. At that, my mother pointed out that it was no wonder that James (and indeed all his brothers as well) were so badly behaved, if he were allowed to be so impertinent with impunity and, whilst she had the floor, she should point out that my wife

---

Divorced parents
Boy 1. How do you like your new father?
Boy 2. He's frightfully nice
Boy 3. Yes we like him too. We had him last year.

never did have any idea of bringing up children anyway. The worm turned and my wife let my mother have a good blast of what she had been inviting for some time. The atmosphere was electric. Eventually, as if nothing had happened, Nigel broke the silence and the tension. 'Dad,' he remarked, 'Bingham says you used to date his Mum.'

P. M. Rossiter

Father comments

Some fifty years ago in a small town in County Durham lived a man whose attitude to education was more forthright than academic. His son was given his term's report by his class teacher at the Junior (Mixed) School, and told to take it home for his father to see at dinner time and to bring it back for the start of afternoon lessons.

As a summary of the rest of the report, the class teacher had written, 'he learns slowly', the report was duly returned with this terse addition from the parent; 'It is your job to learn him quicker'.

Alan Wilkinson

Run away

I must have walked to the station and borrowed money there for a ticket to Waterloo. I do remember, very clearly, arriving at Waterloo, because at that point I made a decision which was later to cause me trouble. I went to the cinema there, which in those days used to show continuous newsreels, not because I wanted to, but because I dreaded going home. How could I possibly explain to my parents why I had 'run away'? Anything to put off that fateful confrontation.

Eventually, of course, I could delay no longer. To my infinite relief my parents were out to dinner, and the servants put me to bed. My mother, however, was summoned home soon enough, and through floods of hysterical tears I told my story. The relief at getting it off my chest was indescribable. I was told not to worry, to have a good night's rest, and she would see what was to be done in the morning.

Unbeknown to me, she then telephoned the headmaster and the conversation – which she recounted to me some years later – went something like this:

My mother: Sorry to be ringing you in the middle of the night, Mr So and So, but I am very worried about Peregrine.

Headmaster: Worried about Peregrine? Why on earth? The dear boy is doing very well. Of course he's fast asleep in the dormitories by now. It's long after the boys' bedtime, you know.

My mother: Fast asleep he may be, but he's not in the dormitory, headmaster, he's right here at home and I suggest you get up to London right away and explain what has been going on.

This the headmaster did, without a moment's delay, and I was woken in the small hours to repeat my story to him. He tried to bluff a bit. Hadn't I been imagining things? etc. In any case, when had I left school? How had I got to the station? He wanted to know the full details. So I told him, not forgetting to mention the newsreel film part. That gave him the opportunity. He turned to my mother with a smile. 'I think, Mrs Worsthorne,' he said, triumphantly, 'Peregrine may have been feeling in need of a little holiday, weren't you, dear boy?'

Peregrine Worsthorne

Sending your daughter to school, 1710

'Sir,

Having a daughter about nine years of age, I would endeavour she might have some education: I mean, such as may be useful, as working well, and a good deportment. In order to do it, I am persuaded to place her at some good boarding school situated in a good air. My wife opposes it, and gives for her greatest reason, that she understands the formalities of visiting and a tea-table so very nicely that none, though much older, can exceed her; and with all these perfections, the girl can scarce thread a needle! but, however, after several arguments we have agreed to be decided by your judgement . . .'

Letter in The Tatler, 1710.

MCP

Father 'I've just asked my secretary to look out a good boarding school for my daughter. If she had been a boy, I'd have had to do it myself.'

Jilly Cooper

More one-upmanship

'My daddy has a Rolls Royce.'
'So what, my daddy's got a yacht.'
'Well, I bet it's not as big as my daddy's yacht.'
'My daddy's got a Rolls Royce and a 50 ft. yacht.'
While an exchange such as the above was going on, one boy kept pretty quiet until, that is, a likely winner had emerged. Then, in a somewhat timid voice, he informed them, 'my daddy owns the Q.E.2.'
(Nigel Broakes' son!)

'Well we have six water beds in our house' led the field. This left one boy totally outclassed and he had to admit to his friends that 'My mummy and daddy only have one bed and they have to share it!'

The Australian

A rude shock
The bursar of a leading public school was well used to receiving distressed or angry responses from his only-too-frequent requests to parents for large increases in the fees.

Unfortunately, on one occasion, his typist erred so that his demand read '... from next September, therefore, fees will be payable at the rate of £4,500 *per anus.*' Back came a letter of weary resignation from one of the fathers: 'Very well – if you insist; but after years of having had to pay through the nose, your latest demand does seem to be unnecessarily harsh.'

Writing home

Boys at modern public schools, no matter what their recurrent complaints, can have little idea how lucky they really are compared with the conditions they might have had to face in the early nineteenth century.

In his youth, Richard Cobden was sent to a particularly wretched boarding school in Yorkshire. He was not allowed home *at all* for five years. He was not even allowed to write to his parents as he liked. Every three months he had to copy out a letter which the headmaster wrote for the boys. This is part of one of them:

> Honoured Parents,
> You cannot tell what rapture I feel at once more having the pleasure of addressing my parents. It has now turned three years since our separation took place and I assure you that I look back with more pleasure to that period than to any other part of my life and I beg to return to you my most sincere thanks for sending me to this school . . .
> your affect. Son
> R. Cobden

Garrett Anderson

A parental visit, 1770

When you receive orders to go into the room where your Parents are, bow, stand still till such Time they bid you sit down, or inform you what is their Pleasure with you . . . sit still, upright and silent; look not at anyone that is in the room . . . so as to stare and ogle at them . . . play not with anything about you viz., Buttons, Handkerchief and the like; put not your Fingers in your Mouth, bite not your Nails, make no Faces . . . make no Noise with your Feet . . . put not your Hands in your Pockets; turn your Toes out, lay not one leg over the other.

If you cannot avoid sneezing or coughing, turn aside and make as little noise

---

Don at Radley 'It is extraordinary how bucolic some of the old boys sound when they come back after a few years.'

Child 1. 'My family used to own most of Bath, but unfortunately they lost it in a game of cards.'

Headmaster of Winchester 'The boys are not rich. In fact most of them are extremely poor. It's their parents who are rich.

Child 1. 'My mother went to Princess Anne's wedding'
Child 2. 'My parents were asked but they didn't want to go'

Jilly Cooper

---

in doing it as you possibly can, it is very vulgar in any one to make a Noise in coughing and sneezing.

You should have a special care not to make any Kind of Faces, that is grinning, winking or putting out your Tongue, and the like, for that will make you despised.

Matthew Towle

How to be a good mother

'Boys are often reasonable, schoolmasters sometimes, parents never.' Thus spake F. W. Walker, the Victorian High Master of St Paul's School; but the years have gone by and parents, especially mothers, have changed. Whether or not they are becoming more reasonable, the reader of these three true stories is invited to judge:

1966 Mother, seeing off her fourteen-year-old son on the school train: 'Here, darling, you'll need this on the journey,' and she pressed into his hand a half bottle of gin. (Why not a full bottle?).

1976 The headmaster of a famous school was showing a visitor round his domain and the latter enquired how much pocket money the boys were allowed. The headmaster suggested that they should ask the next boy they met.

The boy was unable to give a clear answer, so the visitor asked him how much money he had in his pocket. The boy produced his wallet. In it was no money but there were two cheques. The first of these was made out for £100 by the boy's father – the second one signed by the boy's mother was blank. 'Oh, she always leaves it blank,' said the boy, 'so that I can fill it in for more than father gives me.' (Were the Beatles wrong? . . . Can money buy us love?).

1986 A more cheerful story: A boy aged sixteen left his single-sex school after 'O' levels to become a boarder at one of those old public schools that have set fashion and become co-ed in the sixth form. After unpacking on arrival by train he discovered that he had left a number of little things behind, so he rang home and his working mother promised to bring them over in her car next week. When she arrived, everyone at the school seemed to be playing outdoor sports or rushing about and only with difficulty could she even obtain directions to her son's boarding house. She rang doorbells and called out, but nobody answered, so she read the notice-board and made her way to her son's study-bedroom.

When she went in she was rather surprised to find her son in bed with a girl. With commendable *savoir faire* she said: 'Oh darling, I'm sure you shouldn't be doing this.'

'It's quite all right mother,' he replied, 'we're both off games.'

Rodney Exton

The facts of life

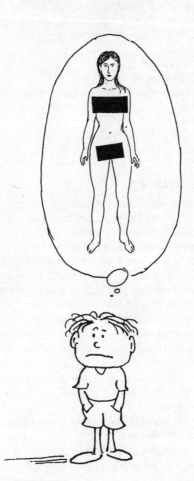

Boys in the mould

Boys must not be allowed to form a distinct society of their own: they are not sent to school to form a society for themselves; they are sent to live in a society framed and governed by the intelligence and virtue of a man whose profession is to train boys. Boys are sent to school, among other purposes, to be instructed in the knowledge of social life, not a social life founded on their own notions, but one which shall be a fit introduction to the social state of manhood.

Quarterly Journal of Education, 1885

Small but wise

I was teaching English to a class of eleven-year-old boys. We were talking about shapes. The children insisted on telling me the shapes that they liked – clouds, trees, buildings. I was becoming rather bored so I stopped the children telling me their favourite shapes and said 'two lines of poetry have just come into my head,

A pretty girl who naked is

Is worth a million statues.'

A small boy in the front row shook his head wisely and said, 'Very true sir, very true'.

J. C. Knapp

Friendly advances

North Foreland Lodge was considered to be the crème de la crème, as Miss Brodie would say, both socially and scholastically. Miss Fennella Gammell, the headmistress, was certainly in a class of her own. She was a tall dark, strikingly handsome woman with her hair swept back into a bun at the nape of her neck; her voice was soft and she commanded respect on sight.

Papa, with his well trained eye for a pretty woman, took a great shine to her. He even stopped ranting and raving about 'MY Italian daughter sent to another blasted English school.'

I really could not be blamed for the first incident at North Foreland. It would never have taken place if my father had not insisted that I should have a bedroom to myself. He always seemed to want me to feel that I was a person apart. Anyway, one evening, just as I was dropping off to sleep, my door handle slowly began to turn. Then by degrees, the door was pushed open. One of the 'Big' girls shut the door silently behind her and, smiling, walked towards my bed.

Stockily-built, with broad shoulders and arms too long for her body, she had straight, chin length hair and I noticed her regular very white teeth as she smiled. Her eyes held mine as she came closer. I pulled up the sheet to my chin, but she took no notice and sat down very close to me. She said nothing

158

THE FACTS OF LIFE

– neither did I. Then gently and very slowly she leant over and pressed her lips on mine. It was so unexpected that I started to scream but her hand clamped firmly across my mouth to muffle any sound. 'You little idiot,' she hissed, 'It would have been such fun,' and with that she was gone. I was bewildered – I was barely ten years old and the sensual side of life was still a closed book. Puberty is such a sensitive, vulnerable stage of one's life, but at that moment and in retrospect, my reactions were instinctively heterosexual.

Katie Boyle

Jagger wants the facts

The principal concern of most of the inmates of Dartford Grammar School was the pursuit of sex. Although Mike could find girls to accompany him to Sports Day it was very difficult to find any real action. But one had to maintain appearances – to have bemoaned, publicly, one's enforced celibacy would have outraged convention.

Carey Schofield

In writing

Of course, what constitutes filth and the mysteries of sex have always been a cause of contention in British schools. An old friend and mentor, Sir Clifford Norton, told me about sex education in Rugby before the First World War. The headmaster, who must have been an enlightened man, summoned all the boys who had reached the age of puberty to his study, and after reassuring himself that the door was firmly secured, made the following brief announcement. 'If you touch it, it will fall off.'

The boys were then invited to file back into their classes, now equipped to face adult life.

Many years later, Britain was still irked by this elusive yet fascinating subject. Arriving at a theatre for a performance of a play of mine, I ran into a fellow actor of our troupe, Cyril Luckham, a true friend and magnificent performer who happens also to have very fair skin and hair. He gave every evidence of having wept. It is always disturbing when grown men are reduced to tears, so I took him aside and asked him tactfully what was the matter. He replied that nothing was the matter apart from laughter which had been racking him intermittently for the past couple of hours, and of course laughter and tears leave very similar after-effects, especially in those of fair pigmentation.

He let me in on the cause of his joy. It was, apparently, the first day of a new term at his son's school. The headmaster, obeying the instructions of a government by now aware of the dangers of ignorance, was compelled to explain the facts of life to those of a certain age-group. The poor man had been rehearsing his speech all through the summer recess, and eventually,

159

in a panic of prudery, unable to bear the sniggers he could already hear in his head, he was reduced to composing a pamphlet, published at his own expense, which every boy found lying on his desk as the new term began.

This pamphlet began with the following words: 'You may have noticed, between your legs . . .'

Peter Ustinov

Mirror image

Like most small boys, I developed the usual healthy interest in the opposite sex. I spent hours wondering what they looked like without their clothes on. The fact that one could see little girls wandering about in local paddling pools, or by the seaside, stark naked, was unimpressive. They were only toddlers, so they didn't count. It was one's contempories at school that one mentally stripped in the playground. I had my first break at the age of eight, when a nubile lady of the same age or maybe she was a year or two older, virtually picked me up in the school holidays, and invited herself round for tea. My mother suggested that we should go upstairs and play in my bedroom after tea; a suggestion which Deirdre Dosworth seized upon

eagerly. You see, I even remember her name. Once upstairs she offered me a tour of inspection. Breathlessly I accepted her offer, and she divested herself of her blouse and vest. 'Those are breasts,' she declared. I was not impressed. I'd seen fat boys in the showers who were bigger than she was. This is probably why, when I was twelve and at a co-educational school in Twickenham, I evolved a plan. Not only were the girls of my age infinitely shaplier by then, but we all used to go to the same public baths for swimming lessons. Our changing rooms were divided by a wooden screen which started at the ceiling but didn't quite reach the ground. There was the kind of gap that enterprising West Indians are said to limbo underneath and so get free. I bought a pocket mirror and instructed my mates to do the same. At the next opportunity, we placed our mirrors and by skilfully tilting them we saw the lot. The following week we were surprised to hear sounds of uncontrolled mirth coming from the other side of the screen. Staring aghast at the floor, we saw a row of mirrors tilted towards us. It wasn't their retaliation that rankled – it was their laughter.

Leslie Crowther

The way of the world

Sydney Smith observed that the only way public schools prevented boys being corrupted by the world was by corrupting them before they got out into it.

John Chandos

1918 – fate worse than death

It was at that time that the sixth form mistress came and made one of the most fateful statements of my life. 'I have come to tell you a very terrible fact. Only one out of ten of you girls can ever hope to marry. This is not a guess of mine. It is a statistical fact. Nearly all the men who might have married you have been killed. You will have to make your way in the world as best you can. The war has made more openings for women than there were before. But there will still be a lot of prejudice. You will have to fight. You will have to struggle.' How right she was. Only one out of every ten of my friends has ever married.

Rosamund Essex

Human history becomes more and more a race between education and catastrophe.

H. G. Wells

My father and myself

My father had sent my brother and me to Rossall School, preparatory and public, in Lancashire, his own territory, partly because he believed it to be a good, healthy, roughish school. It must have been about the year 1912, when I was turned sixteen, that he invited the two of us into the billiard-room for a 'jaw', which could hardly be called 'pi' and which he himself described as 'man to man'.

The precise way he approached this delicate subject I don't recall; I am sure he did it as decently as could be done in the circumstances – the circumstances being that he had left it all rather late. The ground for such intimacies needs some preparation, and in common with many English children of our class and time our education in such matters had been totally neglected. Worse than neglected, I, at least, had been misled and reached my preparatory school supposing that I had been delivered to my parents by a stork, a naivety that won me the ridicule of other boys.

J. R. Ackerley

Birds and bees

There was less to be said for him in my last term when those who were leaving were all sent for to his room in order that, as we came to realize only some years later, he might tell us the facts of life. He began with butterflies, of course we knew about them, went on to bees and then to birds and then he thundered out: 'D'you little nippers know the difference between men and women when they have no clothes.' We were so thunderstruck we all said yes sir and I did too but I had no idea and I remember now he said, 'well that's all right then' and seemed enormously relieved. He went on to say that after what he had said about butterflies and the rest we could work it out for ourselves if we remembered how different men and women were and ended with a warning against unspecified vice so appalling that I was as one who has heard too huge a noise, too vast a something that has not been disclosed; it was too much to take in and I was left, in no wise the worse for not knowing, in a void of unmentionables, or as they say all at sea.

Henry Green

From the Common Room Notice Board in the middle of a cold spell: 'Boys may only skate on water passed by the Headmaster'.

The Dark Ages were the times before electric light was discovered.

'Honi soit qui mal y pense' means 'Honey, I have a sore head'.

'The Saxons fought with conkers at Hastings'.

Nicholas D. Coates

Wednesday wife

Concerned mother: Tell me dear, are you always looked after at school and is matron always available?

Grateful son: Oh yes, they look after us very well here. So far as matron is concerned, she is here every day except Wednesdays.

Curious mother: But what happens if you are ill on a Wednesday?

Ingenuous son: Oh matron is the housemaster's wife on Wednesdays.

Jonathan R. Davis

Poetical porn

When I was at school there was a distinct lack of pornographic material available for the pubescent eye. *Playboy* didn't exist and we were reduced to turning the pages of *Men Only* and I think *Health and Beauty*. One day, however, in the library I chanced upon Byron's *Don Juan*. There are, as you perhaps know, many quarters to this work and my inquisitive eye soon ferreted out assorted erotic references which filled me and my chums with some excitement. We duly, therefore, founded a Byronic society, produced a greeny-yellow tie (not really very appropriate) and I was detailed as founder of the society, to acquire a president. It seemed that as George Bernard Shaw was at that time our most distinguished man of letters, that he would be the most appropriate choice.

I therefore wrote off to him at his home at Ayot St Lawrence – a long deeply obsequious letter asking the great man whether he would honour us with being our first president. Some weeks went by and I finally received one of his famous postcards which read – 'No. GBS.'

Derek Nimmo

Outside interests

One term, during our later period at Harrow when John had successfully transferred from maths to history, he was rather surprised to find his history class assembled and ready in good time for the end-of-the-week period. John taught with his back turned to a large window which overlooked a passageway between two tall drab buildings. The boys always seemed attentive and in a particularly happy frame of mind. This degree of interest continued until one evening a boy in the class made a sound of deep satisfaction. John noticed that all the alert faces had developed smiles, and seemed to be gazing through the window. He turned and saw the view that had held the attention of these seventeen-year-olds for so long. At the window of the house across the passageway were three girls with little or nothing on, making seductive gestures. The house was privately owned, and had recently become a weekend brothel. It was not John's fine, stimulating teaching which had been holding the attention of the form. The brothel was closed immediately.

Daphne Rae

Bussing

Miss Buss and Miss Beale*
Cupid's darts do not feel.
How different from us
Miss Beale and Miss Buss.

Anon

*Famous Headmistresses

Staff antics

I met my future wife at a small preparatory school in Buckinghamshire, where she was a matron and I was a young assistant teacher. Suffice it to say that nature took its course and we fell happily in love.

The headmaster of the said school was a bachelor of some sixty years of age who had been a housemaster at Radley.

On the night in question, Heather and I had been out to a local pub. Returning to school at about 11.30 p.m., we decided that this was the ideal time to practice for the staff three-legged race, due to take place on sports day a week or so later. Consequently, we tied ourselves together in the appropriate fashion and set off at some speed and with a good deal of raucous noise up and down the passage of the main part of the school. After a few minutes of this exercise, we collapsed and fell in a giggling heap underneath the main stair case of the school. The door of the headmaster's room on the first floor was thrown open at this point and the headmaster emerged, pursued by the sound of one of the Beethoven's symphonies played at high volume. Leaning over the bannisters, his moustache bristling, he cast his sternest glare over the sight below and said, obviously with as much force as he could muster, 'Why don't you two go to bed?'

So we did.

H. S. Evers

Sailors at school

I was a boarder at Roedean, on the Sussex coast near Brighton -- still one of the foremost public schools for girls in the country.

Unfortunately, at that time there wasn't a girl in the place – just 200-odd sailors in from sea and undergoing an 8-week course in the use of low power electrics in the remote control of guns and torpedoes. It was the autumn of 1942, I'd already done nearly two years on destroyers, and had been recalled to do this advanced course amidst delightful surroundings.

The fair and female peacetime pupils had been evacuated to Wales, or somewhere safer than the South Coast, and the classrooms modified to suit

the requirements of a naval Torpedo School for the duration. Its only link with the former occupants was that we slept in the same dormitories and on the same bunks that once supported more graceful shapes than ours. And many's the night a restless sailor has wondered whether there might still be a flimsily-clad prefect or two still lurking around the building, daringly seeking adventure with the present occupants.

So much so, that the said restless sailor, his passions inflamed by a canteen pint and a Hedy Lamarr film, has not been able to resist leaning out and pressing the bell-push, one of which was fixed on the wall immediately above each bunk. Below each push was an engraved ivorine lable reading: 'Press the button if you need a mistress for any reason during the night'.

After a short pause, stealthy footsteps would be heard heading towads the dormitory, the door would open quietly, and a form approach the bunk to sit gently on the edge of it.

In a low voice the duty Chief Petty Officer would breathe softly into the restless sailor's ear just what would happen to him, health-wise, if he ever again laid a blankety-blank finger on that blankety-blank-blank bell push during the rest of his blankety-blank-blank-blank stay at Roedean!

Sam Morley

From a school essay

All people should be gentlemen except ladies, but it puts a lot of variety in life if some are not.

Jilly Cooper

Lessons behind the bicycle shed

All tribes have their own approach to sex education. The Bemba in Africa leave it to wise old women, while the Nayar of southern India establish dormatories and tell the young to get on with it. Here in modern Britain we are somewhere between the two.

Traditionally we sent our children into bicycle sheds where tuition was given by their peers without embarrassment. I went to one of Britain's lovelier bicycle sheds and was 'told' by a boy called Phillip Myhill, whose description struck me as far-fetched.

'Oh, come off it, Myhill,' I said.

But the years went by and I saw magazine covers that bore out a good deal of Myhill's exotic theory. At this point his sister, Vera, gave an illustrated guide to the female anatomy in the self-same bicycle shed where this whole journey of wonderment began.

'Frankly, Vera, that is astonishing.'

Then Ginger said he had tried kissing somebody once and it was a complete waste of time. And that was that. At ten, we had acquired all the knowledge on this subject that we wanted or needed.

Sex education was not a problem for us, but it was a terrible problem for adults, and so it remains. Basically, they felt that in some way they should be involved in this tuition, even though they were obviously and chronically incapable of doing so. Some time after the bicycle shed, Ginger's deeply embarrassed dad gave him a book which suggested that rabbits had been talking to Myhill as well.

Poor old adults have been trying to sort out sex education since the early years of the century. It was first mooted in 1914. We know this because that is when the London County Council banned it from all classrooms. The ban was lifted in 1945 when more mooting broke out and continued throughout the 1950s.

What actually happened in the early days was that schools got in an adult from outside because the staff were all too embarrassed to talk about it. At my school we sixteen-year-olds had to endure 'the sex talk' from Commander Bledlow (retired), a man so old that he must have had a prodigious memory to recall anything about the subject at all.

He stood next to a blackboard upon which he drew a map of the female body and, wielding a long stick, discussed the matter as if it were the siege of Jakarta. Sex sounded awful: just a network of incomprehensible tubes that caused disease, unhappiness and unwanted pregnancy.

It never occurred to me that sex was supposed to be pleasant and I saw no reason why I should ever have to do it. Fortunately, the BBC's output consisted almost entirely of naked people in bed together with evident signs of mutual amusement; it was the only clue one was ever given.

Stephen Pile

School
reports

Field Marshal Montgomery

I hurled myself into sport and in little over three years became Captain of the Rugby XV, and in the Cricket XI. The same results were not apparent on the scholastic side. In English I was described as follows:

1902 essays very weak
1903 feeble
1904 very weak; can't write essays
1905 tolerable; his essays are sensible but he has no notion of style
1906 pretty fair

My time at St Paul's was most valuable as my first experience of life in a larger community than was possible in the home. The imprint of a school should be on a boy's character, his habits and qualities, rather than on his capabilities whether they be intellectual or athletic. By the time I left school a very important principle had just begun to penetrate my brain. That was that life is a stern struggle, and a boy has to be able to stand up to the buffeting and set-backs.

John Bratby

The form room was filled with 30 boys of about 15 years of age waiting for the headmaster, a portly man called Mr Dean, to come and comment on the exam results. Mr Dean entered to a respectful silence. He sat by the form-master and studied the papers before him.

Across the form room Mr Dean looked for some time at a boy called Bratby and all the boys looked at Bratby with laughing eyes.

'You are bottom of the form Bratby, I can see you not getting on in life any further than selling peanuts on a street corner outside the Empire cinema in Kingston.'

The whole form erupted with merriment. The boy Bratby was crimson.

Those examinations were in advance of the General School Certificate Examinations.

At the end of the following term the boy Bratby came 5th in the form, spurred on by shame. In the GSC exams he obtained one distinction, five credits, a number of passes and no failures for he had no intention of becoming a peanut vendor.

Charles Darwin

Charles Darwin remembers that the best part of his education at school took place in his spare time, bird and insect watching ('I remember wondering why every gentleman did not become an ornithologist'), and working on chemistry experiments with his brother, which earned him a public rebuke from the headmaster for wasting his time on such useless subjects. 'He called me very unjustly,' says Darwin, 'a "poco curante" and as I did not understand what it meant is seemed to me a fearful reproach.'

John Chandos

Winston Churchill

Winston had never been happy at any of the schools to which he had been sent, nor, with very few exceptions, had he formed a high opinion of any of the masters who taught him. His school reports had been far from satisfactory and had earned for him Lord Randolph's anger and frigid contempt. Winston was therefore apt to take lightly any disagreeable comments in his own son's reports, and was wont to regale Randolph with tales of pedagogic folly and ineptitude, and generally encourage him in saucy opinions about his pastors and masters.

Clementine Churchill

George V

In order to keep track of the daily progress of his pupils, Mr Dalton caused to be printed two large albums, similar to cellar books, in which he recorded their proficiency in the general subjects of the curriculum, adding each Saturday some general remarks on conduct during the week. The album entitled *Journal of Weekly Work, Prince George* is still preserved in the Round Tower at Windsor, bears many astringent comments in Mr Dalton's handwriting. The following extracts covering the Autumn and Winter of the year 1876 may be quoted . . .

September 23. Prince George has been good this week. He shows however too much disposition to find fault with his brother.

October 14. Too fretful; and inclined to be lazy and silly this week.

December 9. The slightest difficulty discourages him.

Harold Nicholson

Harold Nicolson

My dear Family, this is my last letter from Well. Coll. and will be quite historical and figure in my biography when it comes to be written by a devoted wife. I cannot say I am in the least sorry. In work I have succeeded here above my expectations, yet I should not say that I was at the top of the tree. It is so funny to think that it is nearly over and how happy and unhappy

I have been . . . .I shall be sorry to say goodbye to Pollock, Kemp and to Mr. Perkins. They have all done their best for me and I don't think I shall ever forget it. I am beginning to see that brain counts for little but that character counts everything, and it is not a pleasant thought as my character is weak and easily influenced.

Randolph Churchill

During the General Strike, when Randolph was at Eton, he was determined to keep himself abreast of events, writing to his mother:

'At the beginning of the General Strike I asked the 'Sheep' [Colonel Sheepshanks, his housemaster] if I could install a wireless set, in order to hear the news bulletins. However he would not let me. So I have fitted up a secret one in the bottom of my armchair. It works extraordinarily well and I can hear London quite easily . . .'

1820: *Compulsory reports to parents*

My Dear Parents,

We have committed a great sin. For William Denison spat on the usher's back as we went to bed.

I remain,

Your affectionate son,

My Dear Parents,

We have committed a great sin. For we have bought apple tarts without the leave of the Master, when we have plenty to eat and that of the best quality.

I remain, etc.

G. A. Denison

Laurence Olivier

The All Saints' Christmas productions were special affairs. Since the school's choir served numerous churches in London on a voluntary basis, it had become the custom for distinguished parishioners from those churches to attend the annual Christmas productions as a way of expressing their gratitude. On this occasion, no less a personage than Ellen Terry, the aging first lady of the English theatre, was in the audience. At the end of the performance she was expected to go backstage and say something politely praiseworthy to the company and its director. Dutifully, she did so. But in addition, she singled out the eleven-year-old Olivier for special praise. Apparently she was genuinely impressed by his playing of Brutus, for she returned to see the next evening's performance and then made note of it in her diary: 'The small boy who played Brutus is already a great actor,' she wrote.

Thomas Kiernan

Margaret Thatcher

Surprisingly enough, she was never exceptionally clever in class. She nearly always came top of her form in exams, but this was not because of brilliance, but rather through sheer hard work. She was always rather quiet and withdrawn in class; but she was listening and would go away after school and study what she had been taught. The only subject that she was never any good at – and the one subject that cannot be swotted up – was art. Her marks in this tended to bring down her average somewhat but she was nevertheless put up into the 'a' stream after two years, and there she stayed, concentrating on science as she went up the school.

Penny Junor

David Ogilvy

At the age of nine I was sent to board at an aristocratic Dotheboy's Hall in Eastbourne. The headmaster wrote of me: 'He has a distinctly original mind, inclined to argue with his teachers and try to convince them that he is right and the books are wrong; but this perhaps is further proof of his originality'. When I suggested that Napoleon might have been a Dutchman because his brother was King of Holland, the headmaster's wife sent me to bed without supper.

David Ogilvy

Peter Ustinov

In 1939 my report read like this: 'He shows great originality, which must be curbed at all costs.'

Randolph Churchill

Randolph had not been long at Eton when he wrote a thesis on *Women and their Place in the World* which he considered worthy of a leather binding (hence its survival). This thesis begins, 'In dealing with a subject so large and so pressing as to the correct position that should be occupied by women in the world today, it does not seem to us a profitable expedient to trace their history from the neolithic age . . .' Schoolboy Randolph went on the deplore the education of women as it made them 'dull and uninteresting' and he hoped the vote would not be extended to them because 'women are less able than men . . .' and 'the most able women are the least likeable'. Echoing his father's opinion of Lady Astor, he went on, 'Although only one per cent of the House of Commons consists of females it is a woman who is by far the most unpopular member.' Randolph ended his thesis by quoting the resolution made in 1780: 'The influence of women has increased, is increasing and ought to be diminished.'

Evidently his master approved of this diatribe for at the end he wrote in pencil, 'The whole form and arrangement of this is excellent; the treatment is thorough; and with most of the views expressed it is impossible not to sympathize.'

Anita Leslie

Science: I am enclosing the bill for one science laboratory.

Mathematics: 3 and easy, but 2 easily distracted 4 various reasons.

Alan Bullock

I was a bit of a rascal at school as I remember. Always up to tricks. Definitely not one of the 'goodies'.

When I was in the sixth form I was keen on photography and one of my favourite things was to take sneaky photographs of the schoolmaster and the class when they didn't know it, with a little Brownie 2A camera. It was hidden in a small cardboard box with a small hole in the front of it, just big enough to clear the lens. I used to put a school textbook in front of it, and wait for the best moment. It never took too long before something developed in the lesson. I quietly and quickly slid the book to the side and clicked the shutter. I leave it to your imagination as to some of the little gems I managed to snap in secrecy.

We did have some fun times and often at the expense of a pupil. I remember Alan Bullock who was a couple of years older than me. We went to school together and later he went on to become Vice Chancellor of Oxford. During Latin, the master handed back the work we had done the week before, and he always made comments to help us correct our mistakes or sometimes just to encourage us. This particular day Alan Bullock's piece came back with just one word written on it 'Omasum'. Immediately the lesson was over we all gathered round and looked it up and it's a word which means 'bullock's tripe'.

Denis Healey

Debra Hall

I actually went to school in Barbados in the West Indies, between the ages of ten and thirteen. When we went back there on holiday it happened, funnily enough, to coincide with the time of the war in the Falklands, where I had also been to school, which was quite a turbulent time in the world. Anyway, I went back to the school that I had previously been at between ten and thirteen – an impressionable time in our lives, as I'm sure you'll agree. At that stage I was one of about three or four white girls in the class, though I only recognise that now because at the time it was irrelevant. We were all kids together, laughing at anything and learning everything at the same time in the same way, sharing everything.

I went back to visit the headmistress. I could just about remember her as a person but knew somehow that she had something special about her though I wasn't sure what. I suppose I must have been about twenty-six or twenty-seven when I went back, and in the course of chatting to her we talked about a wide range of memories; people we remembered and things that had happened at school, how things had changed, what we were all doing now. All the things you would expect. Then suddenly I found myself saying that what I hadn't appreciated when I was at school, but that I did as I came to grow up, was that I was able to look back on all those years and realise that during all that time I was just not aware in any way, shape or form, of my colour and that of the other girls in the class. We were always a right old mixture: some very black Africans, some very light West Indians and some mid brown girls, and us handful of white ones. But I was only ever referred to as 'the English girl'. I can never remember being described as white. The colour of our skin had no relevance. We were all on the same wavelength, same friendship wavelength and same educational wavelength.

As I was explaining this to the headmistress, just in the middle of our general conversation, I noticed her eyes beginning to fill with tears, and they started to pour down her cheeks. I wondered what on earth I had said to upset her. Then she said to me 'I have worked all my life to hear somebody say that. You have made it worthwhile'.

Larry Adler

In April, 1985, I was invited by the president of the Peabody Conservatory of Music in Baltimore, to be guest of honour at their 90th anniversary celebration. As a gesture of goodwill they sent me my report card from the time when I was a student at the Preparatory School. This report indicated that I was aggressive, uncooperative, didn't practice and was totally lacking in musical ear. I would go along with all of that except the last. I had a good ear, too good because I could pick up and reproduce whatever I heard so

that it seemed unnecessary to practice. Nobody explained to me that Rachmaninoff, Paderewski, Hoffman, great as they were, still practiced.

I was chosen to take part in a student recital and for it I prepared a piece by Grieg, Waltz in A minor. I had the piano score but preferred to imitate Rachmaninoff's recording of it. By recital day I thought my Grieg compared favourably with Rachmaninoff's and I even gave myself a slight edge on Sergei.

When my name (Lawrence Cecil Adler) was called I came out onstage, sat at the piano, but, before I could begin my Grieg, the principal of the Preparatory School siad, 'And what are you going to play, my little man?'

She picked the wrong little man. Then as now I disliked being patronised. I glared at her, registering instant hate, and, instead of the Grieg Waltz, went into a stride version of "Yes, We Have No Bananas".

I didn't get very far into it. While my fellow students were whooping with glee, my choice being an innovation for student recitals, the principal, to quote Wodehouse, was far from gruntled. She stopped me after about 8 bars, to boos from the student audience, and told me to return to my seat. Within a few days my parents received a letter from the principal which said, in effect, don't send him back. I was expelled, a unique distinction that still holds. No other student has ever been expelled from Peabody.

The world, I like to think, lost a budding Rachmaninoff but, for better or worse, it gained a mouth organist.

Robert Powell

Manchester Grammar school has always been recognised as a school with very high academic standards. Hence a placing there as a scholar held a lot of prestige value for any young person lucky enough to get in.

Come my last year at the school and eventually the day when we received our final report. The really important one that gave us our credentials and would or should determine which way we would go. We all hoped for a good report from each of the masters and good character references, but the one we needed most was the comment from our High Master. That year it was Eric James. I was on tenterhooks. How would he assess my potential for the future?

Now imagine, the report sheet had been filled in by all the masters first and at the bottom of the paper was the largest box of all. This section was allotted to that most important gentleman – the High Master.

I gingerly picked at the sealed envelope to get a sneak preview before I got home with the completed report. This one was much neater than all the previous years. I suppose because this was 'the one'. It all looked OK until I noticed that the main box at the bottom was nearly blank except for five little words: 'Very much enjoyed his Lear.'

It knocked me for six, but I smiled, and I still do when I think back to that day. How could I be anything other than an actor after that?

Just a passing thought. On my first day at school I hardly noticed the other skinny little boy who started on the same day as me, until we were seated next to each other in the same class. The years have flown by, and we have both come a long way. Ben Kingsley and I.

I wonder what Eric James made of Ben, and what kind of comment he wrote on his final report?

Dinsdale Landen

When I was about six years old my father was on the board of governors at the small school I attended. I had been up to something or other, and because of my misdemeanour, I was called up before the headmaster. Being one of the governors, Dad was a friend of the Head so he got all the details of the confrontation passed on to him.

I was tidied up and got ready to go to the study, and it all seemed very official to my six-year-old mind. I hadn't met the Head, or if I had I'd forgotten. Of course I knew him from a distance like all the other boys, and I was up to date on all the usual schoolboy gossip about him and his staff. Some time had elapsed since I committed whatever the crime was. I can't *now* recollect what I had done and, more to the point, I remember clearly on the day I couldn't think of anything that might cause me to be in trouble, and so I was quite interested in this visit to see the Head. I certainly thought that the master who was taking me along the corridor needn't have looked so serious. Looking back I must have looked ridiculous, this obliviously happy little boy strolling in to be reprimanded.

Apparently I did most of the talking and the Head never really had a chance to get around to the reason he had needed to see me for in the first instance. He probably forgot what I'd done too. After all, it must have put him off his stroke when this six-year-old kept asking him what it felt like 'to be over a hundred years old.'

School reports
He says he will go down in history. He will also go down in English and Geography.

Tony sets himself very low standards which he then fails to achieve.

Christmas term. Headmaster's comment.
Quite one of the worst reports I have ever read showing the results of truancy, idleness and bad behaviour. He must improve.

Easter Term
Very bad indeed – a great improvement.

'Please sir, what's it actually like to be over A HUNDRED?'
'Gosh sir, imagine, *one hundred years old.*'
'No, even older.'
I think he must have smiled about it afterwards, and I think perhaps he stored it all up until it came to the time for my school leaving report. How about 'misplaced optimism will get Landen nowhere.'

P. G. Wodehouse

He is a most impractical boy . . . often forgetful; he finds difficulty in the most simple things and asks absurd questions, whereas he can understand the more difficult things . . . He has the most distorted ideas about wit and humour; he draws over his books in a most distressing way, and writes foolish rhymes in other people's books. One is obliged to like him in spite of his vagaries.

Benny Green

Sacheveral Sitwell

Ed: During the holidays from Eton.   *Entry in Who's Who*

Dominic's Mother

My son Dominic had the doubtful distinction of attending four different prep schools between the ages of seven and thirteen. Three of these, after long and successful histories, closed down quite co-incidentally soon after my son entered them because of what were called 'financial exigencies'.

One result of having to go through the process of application, inspection and interview several times over was to give me a curious insight into the quirks and idiosyncracies of prep-school Headmasters and their wives.

Of the many strange and improbable characters I met, one however, stands out from all the rest. He ran a very small establishment cramming knowledge into 20 small boys, although in no way did he let it resemble the usual 'crammer'. He was a genuine scholar and an inspired teacher but it pleased him to present himself as a sort of latter-day version of Evelyn Waugh's immortal 'Dr. Fagan'. For some reason he took a liking to me and over the few brief months I knew him before the seemingly inevitable 'financial exigencies' overtook him, he treated me to many confidences.

'Four types of sherry in the cupboard, from tops to cooking, depending on the class of parent' he said to me at our first meeting ensuring the while that I could see the 'Fino' label on the bottle he was pouring.

'Always have at least *one* Rolls in the drive on the first day of term', he pronounced on another occasion, 'lends a bit of tone'.

'How do you manage to ensure that?' I asked.

'Little arrangement with the local undertaker', he replied unabashed.

But perhaps his most princely pronouncement came in his final end of term report:

'I shall now depress you by reviewing Dominic's academic achievements', he wrote. 'In forty years of schoolmastering it has been my experience that any boy with a mother as pretty as his will go on to do well in the world.'

Garrett Anderson

Report writing is taxing. You feel you are doing well if you manage more than twenty reports to the pint. However, the arrival on the scene of the music reports normally raises morale:

'Jason has worked well this term. His grips and positions are good, as are his rudiments. His pieces have really progressed well and his time-keeping is much better. He works well between lessons – as well as in the lessons. Next term we hope to start rolls on the side drum'.

'He can make a very good sound when he is fresh. This gradually gets breathy as he plays. He learns easily and tends to get tired of things before he has really polished them, so more stamina is needed'.

The Australian

The bad
old days

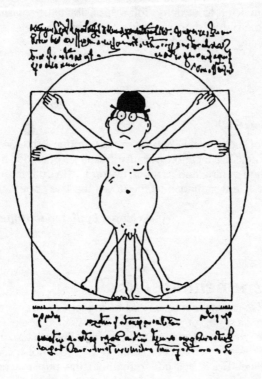

The higher thoughts of Dr Arnold of Rugby

While he was by profession the headmaster of a public school and a teacher of boys, he regarded both the institution and his charges with distaste, because a public school was a society of boys, and Arnold heartily disliked boyhood as a state 'riotous, insolent and annoying to others, like the gaiety of a drunken man'. The unsanctified exuberance of boys was to him 'a spectacle almost more morally distressing than the shouts and gambols of a set of lunatics'. He distrusted and felt aversion to apple-eating animals as a species, his own haunting recollections of schoolboyhood informed him, of 'monstrous evil'. He volunteered confirmation of John Bowdler's notorious but unoriginal remark (borrowed without acknowledgement from Fielding in playful mood): 'I am afraid the fact is, indeed, indisputable. Public schools are, indeed, the very seats and nurseries of vice' and 'none can pass through a public school without tasting too largely of that poisoned bowl' (of 'low base and mischievous principles'), while good qualities brought from home were 'partly corrupted at a public school within a month'. What he saw and felt, with intense personal reminiscence, as the 'evil of boy nature', made him always 'unwilling to undergo the responsibility of advising any man to send his son to a public school', and tempted him to prefer a 'good private tutor', an educational role he had himself essayed.

John Chandos

Pastures new

That sarcasm of eighty years ago of some German professor who said he approved of English education because it was so good for the mind to be 'fallow till the age of nineteen' is much nearer to the truth than supposed. Or it was till these scientists began laying down the law about their intolerable lore.

George Lyttleton to Rupert Hart-Davis

Self-government at school

The reliance of a headmaster upon his boy officers, under whatever title they acted, and the strength of their union, was such that, in an early open collision between the two forces at Eton, in 1768, the sixth form's most potent weapon was a *strike*, a cessation of their normal administrative disciplinary office. Boys' self-government in the public schools persisted because men who had experienced it as boys emerged with a predominantly favourable impression of the system, and sent their own sons to get similar experience. The force of precedent and tradition in public schools might indulge vicious or reckless, or disreputable propensities of temperament. 'Nobody could have guessed,' said Leslie Stephen in a sarcastic sally, 'that an ideal education would be provided by bringing together a few hundred lads and requesting them to govern themselves.' But if 'nobody could have guessed', there were those who could, and did, observe and remember, and draw the conclusion that an identifiable process of evolution took place in boys who remained at a public school long enough to gain seniority and carry its burdens. *The Times* remarked in 1858 that it remained an unsolved problem how 'those fierce passions are tamed, how the licence of unbridled speech is softened into courtesy, how lawlessness becomes discipline . . . and all this within two or three years and with little external assistance', and suggested that 'parents may well abstain from looking too closely at the process and content themselves with the results'.

John Chandos

A fight to the death

'A most awful and horrible warning not to fight in the playing fields happened last night.' Two boys, Charles Wood, and Francis Ashley, the youngest son of the Earl of Shaftesbury, having quarrelled, their respective friends entered into an engagement for the principals to settle their differences in a fight in the afternoon of 2 March. Reports of what happened vary in many particulars, but what is known for certain is that the two boys – Ashley, aged thirteen, and Wood, aged fourteen but considerably bigger – fought for about two and a half hours and at the end of that time they both collapsed. Wood was assisted from the field; Ashley in a state of coma was carried back to his house by two friends and placed on his bed. He never regained consciousness and died that night.

Milnes Gaskell

A leaping bounder

Among the unnumbered anecdotes of this period is one concerning the prank played by a young peer upon Keate's successor, Charles Hawtrey. The boy, who was something of a gymnast, engaged a professional acrobat at Windsor fair to teach him his *pièce de résistance,* a high leap into the air from a stationary position. Once he had mastered the trick he waited until he next incurred the classic penalty and then issued pressing invitations to all his friends to attend the performance. At the appointed hour there was standing room only in the library. As the headmaster delivered the first stroke, the recipient rose in the air with the levitation of a grasshopper and landed several feet from the block. Instantly, Hawtrey was all solicitude. 'I beg your pardon, my lord. Touched some nerve, no doubt. Go home and be quiet. Better send for Mr Ellison.' A few minutes later 'my lord' was celebrating on the river and receiving the congratulations of his friends.

John Chandos

The Headmaster of Litchfield Grammar

He used to beat us unmercifully; he did not distinguish between ignorance and negligence. He would ask a boy a question, without considering whether he had an opportunity of knowing how to answer it. For instance, he would call a boy and ask him the Latin for candle-stick, which the boy could not be expected to know. Now sir, if a boy could answer every question, there would be no need of a master to teach him.

Dr Johnson

Eton in Dr Keate's day (1800s)

Eton was not to be regarded as a school for serious business, but rather a crèche where big children were sent by their parents to be kept out of harm's way and to amuse themselves. Amusements were lawful and unlawful, and in between was a broad area of practices which were officially disallowed but openly tolerated.

J. D. Lewis

The tip staff side

It was hardly to be expected that the masters, who tended to live extravagantly, should be indifferent to money. Masters, and above all the headmaster, accepted tips from boys at the end of a half term in much the same spirit as hotel staff taking tips from departing guests. At Winchester masters claimed 'gratuities' from the boys, and the supplement was added to the bill like a modern service charge, expressly against the statutes but, having become a custom, being allowed by the Visitors. Similarly at Westminster, what had begun as voluntary gifts by boys to masters had been hardened by time, 'the great nursing mother of abuses', into an obligatory practice. At Eton the transactions were conducted with magnificent shamelessness. A two-guinea *douceur* was due to the headmaster from every boy at the end of each half; 'noblemen' – Peers or the sons of Peers – were expected to leave

double or more than that sum; and, at the end of his time at school, etiquette required an Etonian to make a present to the headmaster of at least ten, rising later to fifteen, pounds, which he left in the great man's study after calling to say goodbye. Sometimes, to jog his memory, and to intimate the minimum sum which would be acceptable, a dish, by coincidence already containing a couple of ten-pound bank notes (and perhaps suggestively, one of a larger denomination to hint that more would not be repugnant), stood conspicuously on a table by the door on the same principle as that used by hotel cloakroom attendants today.

John Chandos

* * *

Although masters at smaller schools were badly off, and often actually poor, at large schools, by the 18th century, they could become extremely rich. At Eton, in 1730, the headmaster's salary was sixty-two pounds a year; but there was an unofficial entrance fee of four guineas for the upper school (noblemen double); and every boy gave a tip when he left. In 1763 the headmaster got £411 in tips alone – say £6,000 today. The headmaster of Blundell's is said to have amassed £60,000 in a twenty-three year reign – a marvellous sum.

In general then (there are exceptions), by the end of the 18th century the grammar schools that survived did so partly as a result of their endowments, but to a greater extent as a result of fee-paying pupils; the wealthier the pupils, the wealthier the school, the better it survived. The final flowering of this development, its identification with class, took place in the 19th century, but at any stage it is a development of enormous importance.

Jonathan Gathorne-Hardy

* * *

A letter dated 21 June 1864, from an Etonian, Robert Pierpoint, to his father, gives an account of his expenses at the end of his last half at Eton.

I am afraid you will be surprised at the amount of money I am going to ask for, but it can't be helped; leaving Eton is tremendously expensive.

Headmaster	£10	0	0	Boat	2	0 0
Tutor	15	0	0	Musketry Bill about	2	0 0
House Butler	1	0	0	Musketry Money	1	0 0
Boy's Maid	1	0	0	Book for Mrs Young		10 0
2nd Maid		10	0	Journey Money	3	0 0
Groom		10	0	Packing		10 0
Cook	1	0	0			
Kitchen Maid		10	0		£39	0 0
College Butler		10	0			

Then there are I dare say things that I don't remember, and to leave Eton well, I should be glad if you could make this into about £44 or £45. [Equivalent to not less than £700 sterling today.]

Eton College Chronicle

A kicker at Eton

When we came back at the beginning of one half there appeared at my dame's a smart boy dressed in light blue jacket, faced with velvet, white trousers and waistcoat, with a turned down collar and frills. I spotted him and at once put the question – 'What's your name,' and 'Who's your father?' He replied, 'I am Charles Stuart Vane, Viscount Seaham, and my father is the Marquis of Londonderry.' Upon receipt of this information I kicked him three times, once for Vane, once for Seaham and once for Londonderry.

Rev. William Rogers

Harold Nicolson at Wellington

During the Lent term Queen Victoria paid her last visit to the College, for which she had special affection because of the Prince Consort's part in its foundation. It was the very day on which the Relief of Mafeking was announced. The old Queen drove over from Windsor with Princess Beatrice. The boys were given a whole holiday. In the morning they had rushed about the quadrangles with Union Jacks and streamers cheering Baden Powell. Young Harold had by now either lost or suppressed his pro-Boer sympathies. The Queen on her arrival exchanged her carriage for a wheeled chair, in which she was propelled round the precincts by her Indian servant, the Munshi, in white cotton trousers. The head boy read her a short address. When the time for her departure came the boys accompanied the carriage down Kilometre. Harold caught hold of a mudguard and ran along shouting, 'Hooray! Hooray!' The ancient monarch sat huddled like a round bundle. Her large eyelids blinked behind her gold-rimmed spectacles. The sunshine glinted on the wisps of straw-coloured hair which emerged from under a black bonnet and ribbons. At the College gate the boys stopped running. They watched the carriage bowl along the main road, the coachmen and footmen sitting straight as ramrods above a little parasol of black lace. The boys waved their straw boaters in a last farewell.

James Lees-Milne

Not my type

I am conscious, moreover . . . of a marked distaste for those who have not benefited by a public school education. This distaste is based on no superficial prejudice; it is founded on experience. People who have not endured the restrictive shaping of an English school are apt in after life to be egocentric, formless and inconsiderate. These are irritating faults. They are inclined, also, to show off. This objectionable form of vanity is in turn destructive of the more creative form of intelligence.

Harold Nicolson

Thackeray at Charterhouse

At the very end of his schooldays, during a three-months' illness which also involved the temporary loss of his curling hair and the use of a wig, Thackeray emerged from his sick-bed 'prodigiously increased in stature', having shot up from 5ft. 6in. to his definitive altitude of 6ft. 3in.

'People must have looked astonished at you,' gasped an impressionable young cousin on hearing of this remarkable achievement.

'Oh, I don't know,' Thackeray told him. 'My *coats* looked astonished.'

It wasn't a development which he himself found particularly impressive. '. . . after six feet,' he said, 'it all runs to seed.'

* * *

There was some talk of starting a Charterhouse magazine, *The Carthusian*, which came to nothing, but not before Thackeray had prepared his first contribution, a parody of a sentimental little ditty on *Violets* ('deep blue violets!') by the then popular poetess L. E. L.. Thackeray's robust burlesque was entitled *Cabbages* ('bright green cabbages!'). By private circulation, it brought him as great a reputation as his drawings, and was thought to be very witty indeed by his contemporaries.

Ann Monserrat

A point of honour

Out of school I carried my indiscipline or independence to a pitch that was never suspected of so hardworking and orthodox a student, and which I can still recall with a smile.

I made it a point of honour to attend Ascot races every year, not because I cared in the least for racing, but because it was forbidden and therefore dangerous. It was not forbidden to go, but it was forbidden to be seen in a carriage, which was the only means of getting to Ascot and back – a distance of 7 miles each way – in the interval between the two callings of absence, i.e. about 3.15 p.m. to 6.20 p.m. As a small boy I succeeded in going every year, being usually picked up by some friendly stranger in a carriage or coach.

One year I did better. I was staying out, i.e. was excused from attending school and expected to remain indoors, for some malady or other. I knew that my tutor, Wolley Dod, had gone away on a day's fishing. So I slipped up to Windsor in the morning, introduced myself to an unknown American couple at the White Hart Hotel, and went to Ascot and back in their carriage, spending an entire day most comfortably and undetected at the races.

George Nathaniel Curzon

Running away to school

My schooldays were the happiest, and at the same time the most miserable, days of my life.

Although I was born in my Grandmother's house in the Dewsbury parish of Cleckheaton, I was taken almost at once to live in the tiny village of Gawthorpe near the little town of Ossett which is itself near the city of Wakefield, and it was at Gawthorpe that I first went to school.

This was in 1930, when I was three years and three weeks old. I could read by the time I was four and was able, less than one year later, to take on a regular job: an old lady with failed eyesight paid me a silver threepenny bit for reading to her from a Sunday newspaper. The old lady's husband had been killed, as had so many others, in an accident down the pit, and both of her sons were gone away to live in Canada. I read aloud their infrequent letters, and wrote the old lady's replies.

I was proud of my literary skills, but unable at that age fully to understand why they should be deemed remarkable. I wasn't conscious of having achieved anything, or of having worked towards any goal. It seemed to me that an ability to read and write was like walking and talking and eating and sleeping, a perfectly natural function. Such modesty endured precisely as long as the Age of Innocence.

* * *

We have succeeded, thank goodness, in raising an entire generation for whom the grinding hardships of the Hungry 30s are unimaginable. Came the time of my G.S. entrance exam, I was the eldest of nine children, including two sets of twins, and the constant struggle simply to exist was a burden to be shared by all. There seemed always to be yet another new baby, and my father worked twelve and sometimes fourteen hours a day, so somebody had to stay home and help out with the household chores. That 'somebody' was always me. After my eighth or ninth birthday I was seldom permitted to attend school more than three days each week, usually Mondays, Wednesdays, and Thursdays. I especially hated to miss Art and English classes, and must be one of the very few children in this world who often ran away *to* school.

In spite of all this, and of having been well under age, I passed that 11-plus exam with (by far) the highest marks ever recorded in that County Borough, and so was awarded a special scholarship. Confusion and consternation, with one small boy smack in the middle. On the one hand the education authorities, determined to set me up as a shining example, and on the other hand parents even more determined to see the authorities foiled.

* * *

The over-riding factor at issue had nothing to do with books and uniforms

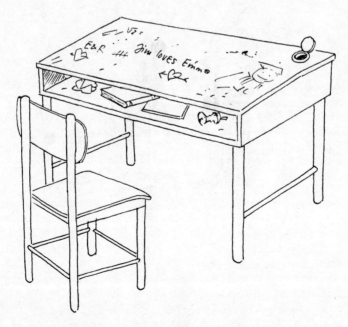

and extra music lessons; it had to do with leaving school at fourteen years old and working and earning and making a valuable contribution to the meagre family budget, as opposed to staying on at grammar school for *at least an extra two years!*

Needless now to say, I never did get to attend the Dewsbury Grammar School. My formal education came to an end at the beginning of March 1941, about two weeks short of my fourteenth birthday. I went to work in Garforth's brickyard quarry in Mirfield, walking six miles there and six miles back every day of a six-day week, and received my first pay packet (£2.15.6) when I was thirteen years and fifty-one weeks old.

School was out for ever. But I still recall, with an ineffable mix of anger and sadness, what utter joy I experienced on those days I was allowed to go.

Angus Ross

Index
of contributors

Quiller Press gratefully acknowledges all those publishers who have generously given permission to quote extracts from their titles. Every effort has been made to trace and to acknowledge all those included in this collection. If there are any omissions, they are regretted.

The publishers would also like to thank Nutmeg Press and Eliot Right Way Books for granting permission to include a number of school jokes from *The Funny Side of School Life* and *The Right Joke for the Right Occasion* respectively.